CW00556363

Goldfish and Fancy Goldfish

Karl-Heinz Bernhardt

We would like to thank the following specialists, companies, breeders and hobbyists for their advice and kindly letting us use their slides. We also thank all those we might have forgotten.

Dandy Oranda's Hideaway, Semmers, Alabama
Mainland Tropical Fish Farm, Singapur
Two Birds Boldfish Farm, Valley Springs, California

Burkhard Kahl	**Alvin B. Lim**
Hans J. Mayland	**Peter Sicka**
Bernhard Teichfischer	**Frank Teigler**
Frank Schäfer	**Kenichi Yamawaki**
Erwin Schraml	**R. Herbst**
J. A. Burke	**Tu Xu Sundries**

Aquarium Glaser GmbH,
for providing beautiful fish for our photographers
from their weekly imports

amtra **- Aquaristik GmbH,**
for providing furnished aquaria
and equipment for testing

Further useful tips about care and maintenance can be found every six weeks in AQUALOG*news*, the unique newspaper for all friends of the hobby.

Read, for example, the latest breeding reports in the news. It is available in German or English and can be obtained at your local pet shop or subscribed to at the publisher.

Order your free specimen copy!

More information about literature you will find at the end of this book on page 47.

Die Deutsche Bibliothek - CIP-Einheitsaufnahme

AQUALOG: *Special* - Serie Ratgeber
Mörfelden-Walldorf: A.C.S.
Goldfish and Fancy Goldfish - 1998

Goldfish and Fancy Goldfish
Karl-Heinz Bernhardt - Mörfelden-Walldorf: A.C.S.
(Aqualog)

ISBN 3 - 931702 - 45 - 6
NE: Bernhardt, Karl-Heinz

© **Copyright by:**   AQUALOG-Verlag GmbH
                         Rothwiesenring 5,
                         D-64546 Mörfelden-Walldorf
                         Germany

Author: Karl-Heinz Bernhardt
Scientific consultant:
Dipl. Biol. Frank Schäfer
Translation:
Shahnaz Durrani-Bernhardt and K.-H. Bernhardt
Index and organisation:
Wolfgang Glaser
Editor:
Dipl. Biol. Frank Schäfer
Cover Layout:
Gabriele Geiß, Büro für Grafik, Frankfurt a.M.

Print, typesetting, processing:
Lithographics: Frank Teigler, Verlag A.C.S.
Bildbearbeitung: Frank Teigler
Prepress/Photo processing/Layout: Bettina Kirsch

Print: Giese-Druck, Offenbach
Printed on EURO ART,
100 % chlorine free paper

 Editors adress:
AQUALOG Verlag GmbH
Liebigstraße 1
D-63110 Rodgau
Phone: +49 (0) 6106 – 64 46 91
Fax: +49 (0) 6106 – 64 46 92
E-mail: acs@aqualog.de
http://www.aqualog.de

PRINTED IN GERMANY

Cover Photos: Calico Fantail (Photo: Archiv A.C.S.), Red capped lionhead (Photo: B. Kahl), Shubunkin, common Goldfish (Photos: F. Teigler, Archiv A.C.S.)
S. 2/3: Goldfish (Photo: Archiv A.C.S.)

Contents

Introducing the Author

The author in his youth in a dormitory of the Peking University during an educational stay in China. On the writing-table you see a goldfish bowl with "fancy goldfish", both from the local market.

Born in 1953, my first focus of interest is said to have been my father's aquarium, before which as a little child I shall have sat for hours. But the first fish which I can really remember were the goldfish my father kept in an aquarium on the landing before the house and the large goldfish in the garden pond of the local ice-cream parlor. Finally I ended up with this first love, even though various other animals took their place in between.

During schooltime I acquired my first aquarium, which later successively was followed by four others. Beside the fish various local amphibians like the smooth newt, yellow-bellied toad and frogs, of course, were also kept from time to time. Most of them had been taken out of the ditches along the fields and a natural pool near the next forest. All the animals, however, were returned after a few weeks, or a couple of years, back to their original waters.

All the aquariums, unfortunately, had to be given up during my military service time. It should be a longer break concerning aquariums, apart from a small exception, of which you shall soon hear. After the military service time I started studying sinology, japanology and Germanics, with a specialization on classic literature. Two study periods were undertaken abroad during this time, one year at the Chinese University of Hong Kong, and two years at Peking University. During the two years in Peking several goldfish were my permanent companions. Due to the lack of a better container they were kept in a goldfish glass on my writing-table. Despite the narrow conditions the fish showed no signs of illness, thanks to the weekly partial water change (with a short stopover in my wash-basin). After the two years the fish were given to an interested university employee.

Another hobby was photography, but unfortunately I took snaps of the animals in China only incidentally. The major interest was pointed towards the cultural monuments, especially to the old monasteries, with the visit of the Shao Lin monastery as one of the biggest highlights. Of course also the landscape and the people in their "typical" surrounding were taken on innumerable films. Nevertheless, many animal portraits, encompassing all genera, were made. If I had only known at that time that some years later the old love for goldfish would again arise vehemently, and, on top of it, two books on them would be produced by me, what could I have visited and photographed, also during two several months long visits to Japan.

After my marriage, shortly after the first child, also the first aquarium came. It was followed by a second child and many more aquariums, as well as terrariums with newts and tortoises from China and Japan. Until today, beside one aquarium with tropical fish, the goldfish, and, of course, my wife and the children remained.

A Chinese praying mantis (Tang-lang), whose movements are imitated in the Tang-lang Kung-fu, one of the multiple styles of this Chinese martial art. Photos: K.-H. Bernhardt

Karl-Heinz Bernhardt

Preface

China is one of the most fascinating countries on earth. Not only the Chinese way of writing is fascinating with its characters thousands of years old, which basically preserved their primary appearance and still are readable today, despite being changed more than once due to changed writing materials and tools. Also, this language is spoken by nearly every sixth inhabitant of this planet.

Furthermore, many important discoveries were made in China, long before one even thought of them in Europe, for instance paper making, black powder, book printing, carp breeding and of course also aquarism. Since almost two thousand years carps were bred in China. From there they later came to Japan, where today's wellknown and popular Koi, this word simply meaning carp, were bred in different colours. They are also known as Nishikigoi, that means "the brocaded carp".

Also the art of landscape gardening was performed there on a high level since long. It

is very wellknown in its miniaturized form in the west, but under its Japanese name, however. The popular 'bonsai' (chinese pen-cai; literally: planted in a pot) originates from China, its culmination are the pen-jing, that means "scenery in the pot" or "potted sceneries". Many other vivid handicrafts, however, are almost unknown to us, e.g. those which yearly are created with the narcissusses. For this purpose jars, stones, the roots, and of course the leaves themselves are used to form the creative characters. The leaves are bent or rolled in certain directions by slightly cutting their edges over a longer or shorter distance.

Known to us, moreover, are several dog races, the Pekingese being the best known

representative. Also, the world's oldest aquarium fish originates from the Middle Kingdom, as far as large ceramic bowls are accepted as the forerunners of today's aquariums. This is the goldfish, or better, the gold gibel, from which all the known types of today's goldfish were bred.

In China, these fish have been kept and bred since many hundreds of years. The numerous types of body shape and colour varieties known today are correspondingly large, and new ones keep adding to them. It is estimated that there are around 300 Chinese breedings, with in addition about 20 to 30 Japanese and a few western ones. On the following pages we want to deal a bit more closely with these interesting fish or personalities, as I almost want to say. Apart from presenting the different varieties, their keeping, reproduction, and diseases, also advice for purchase is given. Many breedings will be presented in the AQUALOG Gold Fish.

In China you often find large contrasts between the modern life and the old traditions. Here you see a farmer with his buffalo ploughing a paddy field. He is wearing a poncho made from a bast like material, in the background we have some tea plantations.

On the left a "sculpture" of living narcissusses on a shelf made from bamboo. Photos: K.-H. Bernhardt

1. General

1.1 Systematics

The goldfish belongs to the carp fishes (Cyprinidae), specifically to the genus of Crusian carps *(Carassius)*, which differ from the common carp and others by the missing barbels. It originates from the Chinese gold gibel, *Carassius auratus auratus* (LINNÉ, 1758), which is also known as the golden Crusian carp. The very same name, *Carassius auratus auratus*, is the scientific name of all the different domesticated forms of the goldfish, since no menbred varieties get a scientific name of their own.

As in common carps and gibels, the first rays of the dorsal fin in goldfish, if present, are longer than the rays of the rest of the fin, which the fin accordingly having a concave shape. Thus the dorsal fin of the goldfish, gold gibel and gibel *(C. a. gibelio)*, a subspecies of the gold gibel found in western Europe, allows an easy differentiation from the true Crusian carp, *Carassius carassius* (LINNÉ, 1758), as the latter does not show any extension in the dorsal fin's front part, and so this fin follows the back line in a convex form.

The second point of differentiation, used mainly by the scientists, is the number of gill rakers. This will not be revealed to the hobbyist even after a deep look into the jaws. The gold gibel and gibel have between 25 – 31 gill rakers, in contrast to 37 – 54 in the Crusian carp.

1.2 History of Breeding Goldfish

The first reports on goldfish, or better on the gold gibel, originate from old China, from the times of the Three Kingdoms (265 – 419). More reliable, however, is a report from the Tang dynasty (619 – 907), in which the appearance of a golden coloured gibel in a lake of Xiu-shui district is noted. For a long period, the catch of this uncommon fish was forbidden as it was considered something special.

The first orange-red gold gibels were discovered during the northern Song dynasty (960 – 1127) around the cities of Jia-xing and Hang-zhou. Already during the southern Song dynasty (1107 – 1187), artificial ponds were constructed to keep and breed the gold gibel. As the Chinese emporer was also interested in their keeping, it soon turned into a hobby of the nobility.

At this time, when common carp breeding in huge ponds had already been practiced for more than thousand years, the specific breeding of the gold gibel in larger facilities was undertaken. Later, for easier selection, the fish were kept and bred in huge ceramic bowls. With this not only the different mutations got a far better chance of survival than in nature but also the breeding targets could be controlled better this way.

While fish with forked or elongated caudal fins, missing dorsal fins or enlarged eyes surely had disadvantages in their daily struggle for survival in natural waters, they now were a point of focus in the ceramic bowls. Their display in the ceramic bowls was pursued since long. Hence, it is understandable why the various stocks of high grade goldfish, like its bigger brothers, the koi carps, should be watched by looking at them from the top rather than from the side.

Since the Ming dynasty (1368 – 1644), the keeping and maintaining of goldfish turned into the maybe most popular hobby of many Chinese, and even today you can buy goldfish and their glasses on the street markets.

In a Ming dynasty book, which was published in 1569, various fin and colour varieties were described. Fish with red, white and blue in varied combinations are mentioned, as well as specimens with three or four lobs of the caudal fin, with telescope eyes, squatty bodies and missing dorsal fins.

During the Qing dynasty (1616 – 1911), the breeding of goldfish reached its zenith. During this period the black, red, purple and calico (mixed coloured) variants, as well as the lion-heads, celestials, bubble-eyes, pearl-scales, and those with narial bouquets (pompons), were created.

1.3 The First Exports

The first goldfish were exported from China to Japan about 1502 and shall have been brought to Osaka and Edo, today's Tokyo. Further exports followed, and the goldfish, which was called "Wakin" in Japan, quickly

The Different Varieties
Varieties and Their Development

became similarly popular as in China and was bred intensively.

In 1643 the first Jesuits arrived in Hangzhou, the centre of goldfish breeding in China. Shortly after, some goldfish were brought from there to Holland. Perhaps it was already in 1611 when these fish reached Portugal, which then would have been the first import to Europe. With certainty, however, the first European goldfish were bred in Amsterdam in 1728.

In France the first goldfish were probably presented in 1755 to Madame Pompadour as a gift. The first provable goldfish reached England not before 1794, however, there may have been earlier imports in 1691 and 1782.

The New World was reached by the goldfish even later. To San Francisco the first goldfish were imported in 1852, and than again in 1874 by Rear Admiral Ammen. However, those fishes will have been most interesting which had been sent to the Chicago world exhibition in 1893 by the Japanese government, as from the surviving fishes of the exhibited specimens the most of all in the west preferred basic type of veiltail was bred.

To Germany, between 1883 and 1885 the goldfish were imported several times by Paul Matte, with which he e.g. bred the famous Matte's goldfish. This was a relatively slender veiltail form with elongated fins, which unfortunately does not exist anymore.

2. The Different Varieties

2.1 Varieties and Their Development

Over the centuries so many forms and colour varieties have been bred that it is not always easy to decide exactly which type you are confronted with. In order to come to a homogeneous subdivision and namegiving it is nevertheless required to set up a certain scheme for classification.

A general classification into goldfish and veil tails, as for example rather common in Germany, is not quite correct. In many cases the Shubunkin and Comets are treated as a third group. In China and Japan, however, all these varieties are named goldfish. The squat forms with enlonged threefold and fourfold

The Matte goldfisch from a photograph around 1895.

caudals are occasionally termed as high quality bred or as fancy goldfish.

Generally, there are various criteria of differentiation, according to which the "classic" forms can be subdivided. Into these the shape of the body, the form of the fins – especially that of the caudal and dorsal fins –, the shape of the head and its skin growth, eyes, narial septum and operculum (gill cover) belong, and, as further criteria, the type of scales and the coloration.

The term "classic forms" used above refers to such forms that have been bred in China and Japan since long time, some of them even since centuries. In recent times, the enormous cross-breedings have led not only to a enormous number of body shape and colour combinations but also to a certain inconvenience of naming these fish. The new Chinese names simply count more or less all the characteristics in a certain sequence, which will cause names like the magpie-coloured-swallow-tailed-dragon-eye. This beautiful fish is described most exactly by this tape-worm name, but will be more likely term as Telescope Panda in the non-Chinese world.

Apart from these "new" Chinese names there also still exist the "traditional" names for many varieties, which often are related to mythological persons or animals or to otherwise important animals. Thus e.g. the common crane with its red patch on the head is also called luck-on-the-head in China, since red is considered as lucky. There it is a symbol of longevity and seen frequently on birthday cards, but also has given name to

The Different Varieties
Origin of the Varieties

Nevertheless, many fish have identical names in Chinese and Japanese. That means, the names are written with the same Chinese characters, which are then pronounced either in Chinese or Japanese.

Apart from this, in Germany occasionally also the English names of the fish are used in the trade. In England and America the different high quality varieties of goldfish are very popular since long. In order to find your way through the complexity of names, the new AQUALOG reference book, beside the German and English names, also contains the Chinese and Japanese terms for the goldfish.

the Red Cranecrown, a white veiltail fish with twin-tail and red growing on its head. This fish we call red cap lion-head or, according to its Japanese name, Tancho Oranda.

Moreover, the various fancy forms have other names in Japan than in China and often the fish to us are known with their Japanese names, despite the fact that originally it might have been Chinese breedings. Generally pure Japanese varieties are named after the place of breeding, i.e. where they were bred for the first time. But in China, the very same fish is, however, known under another name.

2.2 Origin of the Varieties

Most of the old and new types of varieties are not available here or very seldom in the market, as they are extremely expensive and currently (still) have only few fanciers. However, beside a few shops having specialized in goldfish many Koi traders often offer, apart from the coloured carps, some of the few high quality goldfish varieties, so that you can find extraordinary specimens when visiting one. A telephone call beforehand, regarding the current offer, is always advisable.

As already mentioned, not all of the high quality goldfish varieties originate from China. Many types from Japan are equally wellknown, which here are mostly sold under their Japanese names like Shubunkin, Tosakin, Ryukin, etc. The character "kin", pronounced as "gin" at the beginning of a word, which appears in all the above names, means gold and is commonly used as an abbreviation for the goldfish. In Japanese, the goldfish is called ginkyo, and in Chinese

The Different Varieties
Origin of the Varieties

jin-yu. In both cases the same Chinese characters are used.

Further varieties come either from America or from England, where there are many goldfish fans, with some of them having bred new forms during the years. The American Shubunkin, Comet, Bristol Shubunkin and London Shubunkin are worth mentioning here, as well as the veiltail varieties of high quality.

The latter form is associated with a fish having a certain form of caudal fin and should not be taken as the general name for fancy goldfish, as generally done in German speaking countries. Also from England the standard for goldfish breeding and exhibiting originates, generally recognized in the western world.

In Germany not only the good stock of Paul Schäme from Dresden was known very well, but most of all also the above mentioned Matte-veiltail, which had been bred out of many imports between 1883 and 1885, but does not exist today as a pure strain.

Above:
Different interpretations of the character "wen" by various chinese callighraphers, which is supposed to look similar to a goldfish with doubled tail viewed from top.
On the top the oldest form, written with brush and ink, secondly an ancient form, drawn with a style pencil in soft material, the rest very old forms carved in hard material.

Carassius auratus gibelio
Photo: Archiv A.C.S.

2.3 The Varieties in Detail

Already very early people in China began to classify the known varieties into different groups. During the Ming dynasty (1368 – 1644) they differentiated between the wild type gibel, called the gold gibel or the gold carp, and a fish with twin caudal fin, which was named wen-yu. You could translate wen-yu as "patterned goldfish", but it can be taken for sure that this name was chosen particularly because the goldfish with twin-tail, when viewed from top, looks similar to the Chinese character "wen". The name would thus be better translated as "goldfish in the shape of the character wen" or shortened as "wen-shaped goldfish".

In 1848, the great number of varieties caused the Chinese to enlarge the classification groups from three to five. Now all the characters of the various types were differentiated into primary and secondary characters.

The shape of the caudal fin, the form of the eyes and the presence or absence of the dorsal fin belong to the primary characters. Colour, head growth (hoods) and twin anal fins are regarded as secondary. Nowadays, the more recent characters like pearl scales, curled opercula, narial bouquets and bubble eyes are also included in the secondary characters. The narial bouquet is also called pompon or plush-balls.

The five groups mentioned above were :
- gold carp or gold gibel,
- wen-yu,
- dragon-eye,
- dragon-back,
- eggfish.

The form of the eyes named as telescope or globe-eyes in the west is known in China more poetically as dragon-eyes. The dragon was the most important of the mythic animals in China, and as such an attribute for everything imperial. Since the dragon-back apparently is an eggfish with dragon-eyes, the primary character enlarged eyes does appear within two groups in this classification. Therefore in many books this type is not even mentioned.

In recent times the originally primary character dragon-eye is from time to time included in the secondary characters. I can only agree with this new arrangement and recommend the dragon-eyes not to be classified in a group of their own. They should be considered as an additional character with a certain type of variety, as it has always been the case with the bubble-eyes and the celestials.

Thus there remain three large groups of goldfish, as they will be arranged and dealt with in the AQUALOG reference book Goldfish:
- carp-shaped,
- wen-yu-shaped and
- egg-shaped

But now let us investigate the different varieties in detail. To differentiate and classify the types the body shape, caudal fin, dorsal fin, eyes, narial septum, operculum (gill cover), squamation, and the colour are used. In the following we want to take a short look on these characters, more detailed informations will be found in the AQUALOG book just mentioned.

Regarding the **body shape** we can differentiate four types, which are:
- **normal**
  goldfish, Shubunkin, Comet
- **egg-shaped**
  wen-yu type, eggfish, lion-head, Ranchu
- **high-backed**
  Ryukin
- **almost sphere-shaped**
  English and American varieties like veiltail and broadtail.

Possibly an unique mutation with a threefold caudal fin. Occasionally you may find plenty of interim forms among goldfish with paired caudal fins, like the triangle or tripod forms with one dorsal lobe and two ventral ones. This should not be confused with the triple form, were the two caudals are grown together at their dorsal edge. Personally I kept a fish were one side of the paired caudal fin was normal, while the other side showed the tripod form, thus having a total of two upper and three lower lobes. Photo (around 1895) from "La Nature"

The Different Varieties
The Varieties in Detail

Two different forms of squamation: on the top a Shubunkin of the transparent or matt form, appearing almost scaleless, below a Calico Fantail of the mottled or nacreous form.
Photos: F. Teigler, A.C.S.

The latter is a type of a veiltail with a broadened, unforked *caudal fin.*

The largest variation is found, as expected, in the shape of the caudal fin. We differentiate between the

- *normal*
  goldfish and London Shubunkin
- *elongated*
  swallow-tail, Comet, Bristol Shubunkin and nymph
- *duplicated* and
- *missing*
  Meteor

caudal fin, with the duplicated form so variable that this led to a further subdivision.

According to the way how both flaps of the caudal fin are grown together at the upper edge, they can be

- *undivided (threefold),*
  Tosakin, pinched tail
- *partially divided,*
  cherryblossom tail
- *completely divided.*

The largest variation in form is found within the group with completely divided twin-flaps of the caudal fin. Here we differentiate the forms:

- *short,*
  lion-head, Oranda and Ranchu
- *spread out,*
  peacock-tail or Jikin
- *elongated* and
- *largely elongated.*

The two flaps of the caudal fin of the last two types can show a more or less prominent indentation.The elongated caudal fin is

- *simple, barely forked and less spread*
  butterfly tail
- *or quite long and forklike spread or folded,*
  fantail

and the largely elongated form is

- *trailing and not forked*
  old type, broadtail, Broadtail Moor
- *slightly lobed*
  veiltail
- *prominently forked (fourfold fin)*
  fringetail, Phoenix.

All the other characters, still to be detailed, allow to be explained more easily. For the moment we remain at the finnage and take a short look at the *anal fin.*

Short, because there are only three types to mention:

- *single,*
- *double* and
- *missing.*

However, this has no importance for the classification. A double anal fin is desirable, which should be considered especially when selecting fish for breeding. Worth mentioning also is the fact, that a double or missing anal fin usually occurs only amongst varieties with twin-tails, while the single anal fin is not restricted to any type.

The *dorsal fin* belongs to the primary characters, even with also only three forms to be mentioned. These are

- *normal dorsal fin*
  fantail, peacock-tail, Tosakin, perlscale
- *extended dorsal fin*
  veiltail, Moor and other dragon-eyes, Dutch lion-head or Oranda, red cap Oranda or Tancho Oranda, Tosakin
- *missing dorsal fin*
  lion-head, Ranchu, celestial, bubble-eye, narial bouquet, eggphoenix.

A further important character is the *head-shape,* even when it is listed under the secondary ones. The head can be

The Different Varieties
The Varieties in Detail

A pond with the pale bluish type of the Shubunkin, a Japanese word which actually means vermillion patterned gold(fish). Photo: B. Teichfischer

■ **normally flat**
  goldfish, Shubunkin, Jikin or peacock-tail
■ **pointed (mouse head)**
  Ryukin
■ **broad, without hood development**
  toad head, bubble-eye
■ **broad, with hood development**
  high headed types.

The hood development, an abnormal growth of cuticular tissue on the head, cheeks and opercula, is very much appreciated in China, and the whole group is named the "high-headed". As you surely have guessed by now, this group is further divided according to the

form of the skin growth, and we differentiate between
■ goose-head or cap fish
■ tiger-head and
■ lion-head or Oranda.

The skin growth of the goose-head, better known as cap fish to us, is limited to the top of the head only. If it is spread equally all over the head, but moderate in its growth, we have a tiger-head and if it, in addition, is enlarged on the top of the head like a hood, the fish is called a lion-head, also known as Oranda. In the modern variety, these differences are, however, often not very prominent and hence not always easy to recognize.

Oranda is the abbreviation of the Japanese name Oranda Shishigashira, which means Dutch lion-head. This name is somehow misleading, since it does not refer to a variety bred in the Netherlands. Rather it is to be traced back to its import by a Dutch merchant or through a Dutch trading station in Nagasaki, respectively. Often the goose-head or cap fish is termed wrongly as Oranda.

Similarly, a secondary character is the *form of the eyes,* but the dragon-eyes found within this group were formerly considered as a primary character, as mentioned above. Their differentiation according to their shape is as follows :

Pond in the goldfish pagoda, a park in Hong Kong especially created for goldfish. Photo: A. Lim

The Different Varieties
The Varieties in Detail

- normal fish, without peculiar eyes,
- dragon-eyes or telescop-eyes,
- celestials,
- globe-(bubble-)eyes and
- toadheads.

The toadhead is actually a bubble-eye with weakly developed bubbles.

The last two secondary characters, referring to the shape of the body, are based on relatively young varieties. To these the forms with the *narial septum,* some cartilaginous tissue in the nostrils, belong, where we differentiate between the normal and barely enlarged septum and those fish with excessive growth of the septum. These enlarged septa are called narial bouquets, pompons or simply plush-balls.

The pompons always occur in pairs, either two (one for every narial septum) or four (two for every nasal septum). Their colour can match with that of the rest of the body or be in contrast to it. Fish with darker body colour like black, blue, brown or bronze with red to pale red or white pompons are of course much preferred, if you generally like it.

The other character is related to the *opercula (gill covers),* which are either normal or curved at the ends. In their extreme appearance the opercula are totally bent to the front and the gills are completely visible. This form, known as curled opercula, is however not much appreciated here and imported very seldom.

Two secondary characters remain to be discussed, which both are not related to the shape of the body but to its appearance, as is the squamation and the coloration. The *scales* are little bony plates, embedded in the derma, i.e. the deeper layer of the skin. A reflective tissue, caused by guanine particles (iridocytes), which is found in multiple layers directly under the scales and deeper in the skin causes the usually metallic luster of the scales. If this guanine layer is missing, the fish appears lustreless or transparent, almost scaleless. This type is called matt. Both the normal metallic and the matt type of squamation are dominant hereditary characters. The cross between normal and matt scaled fish results in a nacre-like sheen in the fishes appearance, which is termed nacreous or sometimes mottled.

Another effect, called pearlscale, is caused by additional calcium carbonate, which is

deposited on the scales. As a result they appear as halved pearls and are harder than the normal scales, giving the fish's colour a tendency to pastel shading. If such a scale is lost, for example by handling the fish with a net, it will be replaced by a normal scale and disturb the fish's appearance. The pearlscales are a relatively modern character, while the lustreless or matt squamation is known in China since about 1596.

Another, relatively recent variation is the netlike or mock-metallic form. Here the guanine is deposited mainly under the scales and is lacking around them as on the opercula. The combination of this mock-metallic with matt is supposed to result in very colourful, matt fish, called pseudo-matt.

Accordingly we differentiate the following five groups of fish with
- normal or metallic,
- matt or pseudo-matt,
- nacreous or mottled, and
- mock-metallic (netlike) scales, as well as
- the pearlscale.

Above a carp-like goldfish with paired, maybe threefold tail on an old chinese ink painting found in the book 'Histoire Naturelle des Dorades de la Chine' by Billardon de Sauvigny (Paris 1780). Photo: E. Schraml

On the left two carp-like goldfish, a Sarasa with red rings around the eyeballs and a yellow fish with threefold tail. Photo: K.-H. Bernhardt

Finally we come to the *coloration,* for which various pigment cells are responsible, most probably four of them. Each of these pigments, according to its place in the skin and its lacking or mixing with others, creates different colours. These are black (melanophores), yellow (xanthophores), red (erythrophores) and orange (lipochrom) pigment cells.

In the wild type, the gibel, the orange and red pigments are lacking. Only the black melanophores and the yellow xanthophores are present and thus give the fish its silver-grey colour.

In the white goldfish all four types of pigment cells are lacking. If the guanine layer (iridocytes) is present, the fish is silverish-white, but if it's lacking, it appears transparent. But only if the colour pigment is lacking also in the iris and the eye appears red you can speak of an albino. By the way, completely white fish are quite rare, as white is the traditional Chinese mourning colour. Therefore, fish with this colour were not much appreciated and usually were selected when appearing in the offspring. However, nowadays you occasionally get also the white coloured or rather colourless fish from the People's Republic of China, as there they do not pay too much importance to such burgeouise traditions.

If only red pigments are present, the fish appears in a rich red colour, while, if only the yellow pigments are present, depending upon the depth in which they lie embedded in the skin, the fish appears yellow, gold or orange. As with white also the yellow colour has its history; yellow was the imperial colour and thus reserved only for the emperor. Therefore, this colour strain, like the white, was not bred in old China and is still relatively seldom today.

Also with the black pigment cells the position causes the colour tone. If the pigment is found more in the upper layers, the fish appears jet-black, but if the pigment cells lie embedded deeper, the resulting colour is bluish to bluish-black. The ironlike and bronze colouring results from a mixture of black and yellow pigment cells.

Beside the mixture of various pigments to new colours individual colour pigments can also be restricted to certain parts of the body, through which the bi-, tri- and multi-colour variieties developed.

A somewhat independent position is taken by a coloration which is named "pentacolour" (wu hua, literally fivefold patterned) by the Chinese. It could be translated as variegated patterned as well, since five in China was the number expressing completeness or perfection, like the five primary elements, the five sacred mountains, the five directions (including the centre), the five senses, etc. In Japan and in the English speaking world this coloration is better known as calico, a name which is also used in German speaking countries. Even though I would prefer the terms pentacolour or variegated, I will use the common term for simplicity reasons.

The coloration of the pentacolour – sorry, of the calico – is composed of red, black, blue, white and orange, which have further variations through the appearance of metallic and transparent (matt) scales. There are fish with a largely white to bluish-white basic colour and such with an equal mixture of four colours, covered with a pattern of black polka-dots or stripes.

By the way, the coloration of the area around the eyeball can differ from the rest of the body and is variable in the different varieties. The pupil, however, is always black, except in pure albinos.

In the Shubunkin, a carp-like fish with calico coloration, a black ring around the eye is much appreciated, since the eye, together with the black pupil, will thus appear much larger. Also in other calico coloured types this black ring often occurs, while in the black or bluish-black types this is the normal coloration, more rarely we find a fish with a golden ring around the eye.

Amongst the various other types red, golden-red to golden rings surrounding the eyeball are found, while a blue ring rarely occurs and also is less desirable. Quite seldom, too, and equally undesired are fish with one red and one blue coloured ring around the eye.

Completely independent from the coloration of the parents, however, all young goldfish are almost colourless after hatching and appear in a pale grey, which gradually becomes darker, until after about one month the fry appear almost black. Another month later the colour on the belly gets lighter, until the final coloration is attained. This colour change is caused by an enzymic destruction of certain pigment cells. Accordingly these three main colour lines may be distinguished:

- uni-coloured fish
  red, orange, blue, bronze, chocolate brown, iron-like and black
- bi-coloured fish
  red & white, red & black, red & bronze, blue & bronze, and black & white
- multi-coloured fish
  red-blue-white, red-black-white, blue-black-white and variegated (calico)with white, orange, red, blue and black.

3. Keeping Goldfish

First of all you have to decide whether you want to keep the goldfish in an outdoor pond or in an aquarium. Due to its unpretentious keeping the simple goldfish varieties are ideal fish for the beginners, both in an aquarium or a pond. The high quality breeds, generally known as fancy goldfish, however, are a little pretentious to keep and hence not necessarily suitable for the pond or a beginner's first aquarium.

The simple goldfish in its different colours as well as the form with elongated caudal fin named Comet and the Shubunkin are best suitable for keeping in a pond the whole year round and their hibernation in the pond doesn't cause problems. While this is valid for middle European countries, it might be different for countries with a milder or colder climate. These goldfish can be kept in aquariums as well, but you should remember that, under optimal keeping conditions and with enough space, the carp-shaped types can reach a length of 30–35 cm. A minimum length of 150 cm for the tank is hence essential, unless you plan only to keep the juvenile fish in it up to a certain length and then want to transfer them into a pond.

The more delicate fancy goldfish varieties, which still might reach a body-length between 15 and 25 cm, generally require higher temperatures and react more sensitive upon wrong or changing water conditions. Keeping them in a garden pond is thus more difficult and in no case in colder areas they can be left in such ones over the winter period. Also an occasional success, particularly during a mild winter, does not contradict this rule. As they do not attain the length of the simple goldfish, these types are

more suitable for being kept in an aquarium. However, you must take care that the aquarium is not too small and, foremost, is high enough. For some of the fish a 100 litre aquarium is an absolutely minimum. The ideal aquarium should have a length of 150 cm, a height of 50–70 cm and a depth of 40–50 cm.

If possible, aquarium kept fish should be transferred to the garden pond during the summer season. The fish, especially for breeding purposes, can be kept in small plastic ponds or, as in their native country, in large ceramic, wooden or plastic bowls. To prevent too great temperature fluctuations, the bowls are best dug into the ground. The fish become more healthy and thus more resistant and are not too sensitive to diseases. Additionally, their coloration intensifies, especially if the bottom and the sides of the container are coloured dark. The goldfish tends to adapt somewhat to a darker background. If the sourrounding has lighter colours, the fish shows paler colours.

Red and white and Calico Eggfish with narial bouquet. At the upper fish the mottled or nacreous squamation is seen nicely as in the lower one the red ring around the eyeballs. Photo: H. J. Mayland

A white goldfish with transparent or matt squamation. You can see the black ring around the eyeballs very well. Photo: F. Teigler, A.C.S.

3.1 Outdoor Pond Keeping

Unfortunately the setting up of a garden pond cannot be dealt with in detail in the narrow frame of this booklet, but there is enough literature on this matter on the market. However, two points have especially to be paid attention to and shall be described herein. First, the partial shading of the pond to prevent strong sunshine and second, the protection of the fish against cats and herons.

If the fish are only kept in the garden during summer, then a shading during the hot hours is particularly important. With growing temperatures, the water loses its ability to solve oxygen. Therefore in too warm pond-water the fish mostly swim at the surface, in order to gasp for breath. If you additionally have an excessive growth of algae, you will loose fish quite certainly.

Straw-mats are an easy method to provide shade for the pond, as well as they are easy to remove. This method can be used for large garden ponds as well, even though, for a better look, provision of shade by the surrounding vegetation is much preferrable and more natural.

Chiefly various types of bamboo, directly around the pond, are suitable for this purpose, and in addition they add an Asian flair. Nevertheless it should be mentioned, that bamboo is no marsh plant, as sometimes assumed, although it requires a relatively high amount of water, which it clearly shows by otherways curling its leaves.

Also shorter trees and shrubs are suitable, planted at a shorter distance in the south or southwest of the pond. All kinds of (Japanese) conifers are suitable for this purpose; if there are no leaves, no leaves have to be removed from the pond in autumn. If the pond is still under construction this is very easy to be taken into consideration.

A small disadvantage of the natural shade around the pond edges has already been mentioned. During the autumn, increasing numbers of leaves fall on the water surface, later they sink to the bottom of the pond. The leaves begin to rotten when the temperature increases during springtime and thus deteriorate the quality of the water and the living conditions for the fish, because they reduce the oxygen content essential for

their live and eutrophicate the pond. This may, however, be prevented by removing the leaves in time. You can also fix a net over the pond or the part of it which is affected. Unfortunately, the dry bamboo leaves get rolled up and often fall through such nets, then they are difficult to remove.

It's a little more difficult to keep out cats and herons. In Germany, for example, the common heron is legally protected since years, and its number is increasing. It seems to have a preference for the easy to catch goldfish. It has been reported to me from various sources that common herons systematically fished the garden ponds of several villages in the Rhine plains.

As the herons prefer to fish while standing in shallow water, you can easily cover this area with nylon ropes, that prevents the herons from landing there. Also, you should not shade the shallow water area as it then will become more frequented by the fish during intensive sunshine. The easiest way is to separate the areas with shallow water in a way that the goldfish cannot enter them.

The installation of a plastic dummy to keep away the herons, such as are sold in the shops, appear to be questionable, as not all herons keep away from the "occupied" hunting grounds. Personally I was able to watch a heron which stood next to such an imitation and watched out for its prey.

In contrast to herons cats avoid the shallow water and prefer to fish from the dry edge of the pond. These apparently hydrophobic animals lay down on the stones at the edge of the pond and let the front of their paws hang into the water. If your goldfish or kois are not shy and often get food out of the hand, they are especially endangered. However, here I also already watched some cats which, while hunting for frogs, crossed the whole riparian area not minding wet paws at all.

Although these two potential enemies of our goldfish show quite different hunting techniques, the solution of this problem is quite simple, especially in the country-side or the suburbs of big cities, where both animals are prevalent. The border of the pond can be constructed with rocks or stones and the water level should be 25–30 cm below those.

This may not meet everybodies ideas of a naturelike garden biotope, but in such a

Keeping Goldfish in the Aquarium

pond, in which a rich and much variegated plantation is desired, you anyway should keep only very few fish, or even none at all. On the other hand, pond edges constructed with attractive natural rocks, as often found in Japanese gardens, can make a real desirable pond, thus providing protection for our fish pets against the predators. In an affiliated biotope or naturlike pond with dense vegetation you additionally can create a good supplement to the goldfish pond.

3.2 Keeping Goldfish in the Aquarium

Before you purchase your new pets, a suitable home for them is required. If you are already possessing an aquarium this advice is a little bit too late and before being annoyed, you better pass over this part.

Selecting an aquarium, many factors have to be taken into consideration. The most important, however, remains the available place which determines the size of the aquarium. But, is the available place also the right one? If the aquarium on the chosen place is exposed to direct sunshine for hours, then certainly not! The rearrangement of the furniture should then be considered by removing all furniture in your mind and then finding the best place possible. Surely a better and larger place can be found for the aquarium to be bought. It can, however, not be the theme of this booklet to consider what happens to the spare furniture, now remaining.

To be serious again, there is an old saying: the larger an aquarium, the easier its care. No rules without exceptions, you might think. But the exception is rather the Dutch plant-aquarium and not the cabinet, which now perhaps must be moved to the attic or cellar. Additionally a Dutch plant-aquarium is the most impossible to be thought of for the goldfish, whose nutrition consists to a large extent upon plants. Nevertheless, you don't necessarily have to renounce on plants, as we will see below.

But now let's come back to the size of the tank. In larger tanks the fish have more space to swim and with suitable plantation and filtering, the water quality can be controlled and stabilized more easily. The plantation in the goldfish aquarium is a bit more problematic than in an aquarium with non plant eating types of fish, as I just have pointed towards, but its not an impossible attempt.

That leaves us with the swim space. You surely too prefer to swim one lane in a 50 m basin than five lanes in a ten meter pool. It depends upon the plants, you think? Please don't make side manouvres. A roughly rule for keeping healthy fish says: five litres water per one centimeter fish. The caudal fin has to be included, cheating is not allowed. Thus, the pollution of the water is kept under control, a proper filtering included, and the eventually occurring diseases are prevented. Sooner or later, one deviates from this rule, as this is a roughly rule anyway and our fish do not know it and maybe grow beyond the givens.

For instance, thinking of four nice robust Ranchus, (which, by the way, in Japan are compared with Sumo wrestlers), which can attain a length of 15–18 cm, the water requirement would be 300–360 litres. According to the above proposed size of the aquarium, with the length of 150 cm, the required height and depth both would be 50 cm. If the depth is increased to 50 cm and the height to 70 cm, with 525 litres water we would have space for seven adult Ranchus. It could almost be a consolation that the Ranchu is seldom available in Germany, particularly in this size. In England and the United States the situation is much better, and in the States you even can select and order the fish via video.

If the aquarium is used only as a winter quarter for the pond fish, then too much swimming space is not required. Feeding at a water temperature below 10°C is not necessary, as the fish cannot digest the food in cool temperatures. Moreover, the fish reduce most of their activity with such temperatures.

Also for the first aquarium for your daughter or son, which shall be devoted to goldfish, a reduction in size of the aquarium can be made. The simple goldfish, Shubunkin or the plain red veiltail come into consideration as its inhabitants, as they are the easiest to keep. Although the first two types can grow quite large, they nevertheless are available in different sizes from 4–5 cm upwards each spring. Corresponding to the size of the aquarium they grow slower and

Keeping Goldfish
Decoration and Plants

A pair of Tancho Calico or Redcaped Fantail, which are kept outdoor in a planted plastic bowl during summer.

Goldfish pond surrounded by bamboo. The picture is taken on the property of Hottonia e.V., the aquaristic club in Darmstadt/Germany. Photos: F. Schäfer

can be held for one or two years in a one meter long aquarium. Later they can be transferred to a pond, provided there is one, or be given to an acquaintance with a goldfish pond. In no case these fish should be released into open waters. Not that they don't have a chance to survive, but it is forbidden as illegal faunal falsification.

If the place and size of the aquarium have been chosen, the next step is its decoration.

In my opinion this step, along with the setting-in of the first fish and their first progeny, is the most exciting one in the whole aquarism, as you can create a landscape according to your own ideas (although not all attempts lead to success). There are plenty of books available on the set-up of an aquarium, therefore I shall be brief, as is has taken enough time to convince you setting up a large aquarium.

It is obvious that the aquarium must stand absolutely horizontal on a stable shelf, with a soft pad on the shelf, instead of the tiny pebbles, which are to form its future bottom, also that the gravel has to be washed thoroughly first. If every thing is at hand, then the next step can be made.

3.3 Decoration and Plants

Just as with the water conditions, goldfish are modesty regarding the decoration of a pond or an aquarium. More than anything else we ourselves, the fanciers, want to create a small landscape to satisfy our aesthetic demands.

One of the most important points that must be kept in mind when setting up the future home of our goldfish is the fact, that the goldfish, like the other carps as well, love to dredge the ground, i.e. to burrow through the bottom ground more or less intensively. Therefore, the bottom should neither consist of too small or too large gravel. The larger the fish are, the larger the gravel can be, but it never should be sharply edged.

Personally I keep big red dragoneyes (telescope) in an aquarium with a gravel granulation measuring between 5 and 8 mm, and the fish really love to dig the bottom. In the fish pond, however, you best should do without it and instead put the plants in fine-meshed baskets, which are covered with a layer of pebbles.

Although it is quite correct, as suggested in the literature, to slope the gravel layer towards the filter, the goldfish, however, do not care much for this necessity and level it all out within a few days. Hence, you can save the work as it's not worth the trouble. It is more appropriate to terrace the bottom with various stones or large slabs of slate, all of which must not have sharp edges or corners. This allows to form a manifold landscape. The

20 AQUALOG *Special* Goldfish and Fancy Goldfish   © AQUALOG Verlag GmbH

Keeping Goldfish
Decoration and Plants

large stones must not be laid on the bare glass, but on a thin layer of sponge or styrofoam instead.

The plantation is a little more problematic, as every green is considered as diet or is thoroughly investigated if it's edible. The goldfish, like its relative, the carp, is omnivorous and plants form a large part of its diet. This factor should be included in the feeding programme, as explained below.

As plants only the robust ones should be chosen, especially those which are not preferred as food. Also, they should have sufficient time to get firmly rooted into the bottom. By the way, adding any kind of fertiliser to new grounds is not required as they get plenty of it after the fish are placed into the aquarium.

The thick leaved (Canadian) waterweed *(Egeria densa)* and the common hornwort *(Ceratophyllum demersum)*, known to the Chinese as the goldfish weed, have proved to be good in this respect. Nevertheless, the larger fish can still eat their leaves, sometimes right down to the stalk. But these plants are quick growers and have anyway to be shortened time and again and planted anew into the ground. I have made good experiences with different species of Cryptocoryne, if the water temperature during winter times isn't too low.

Plants with robust leaves, like the various types of spear-leaves *(Anubias spec.)* or the water-lilies *(Crinum spec.)* with their leathery leaves, are suitable. Still the young and soft leaves can be bitten and torn.The real tough javafern *(Microsorium pteropus)*, javamoss *(Vesicularia dubyana)* and varied floating plants, like the horn fern *(Ceratopteris spec.)*, the water hyacinth *(Eichhornia crassipes)* as well as the tropical duckweed or water lettuce *(Pistia stratiotes)* remain unaffected.

However, the fine roots of the floating plants get often nibbled away.

In the literature often such plants as Carolina-water-shield/target *(Cabomba caroliniana)*, arrow-leaf types *(Sagittaria spec.)* or vallisnerias *(Vallisneria spec)* are suggested, which however are considered as preferred food and even the coarse type of giant vallisnerias *(Vallisneria gigantea)* had no chance to survive in the same aquarium as my fish.

In the Chinese literature, the water plantain, similar to Ottelia *(Ottelia alismoides)*, is mentioned as a suitable plant. It is widespread in the tropical and sub-tropical

In the Yu quan park, the botanical garden of Hang-zhou:

Above a pavillon at a pond with carps and golden carps.

Various fancy goldfish. On the left being exposed in a ceramic bowl, on the right, the fish from the exhibition collected in a bucket after closing-time to be transferred back to their quarters.
Photos: K.-H. Bernhardt

regions of Africa, Asia and also South China. This plant is rarely available on the market and also described as extremely difficult to keep, thus hardly coming into question as a plant for our goldfish aquarium.

The selection of plants for the garden-pond is much less problematic as the plants of the shallow banks grow preferrably on top of the water surface and those floating free are very tough and not very palatible. For these areas various types of water-lilies (*Nymphaea* spec. and *Nuphar* spec.) are suitable, even if the young leaves may be gnawed at from time to time. Further suitable plants are the water sword-lilies *(Iris pseudacornus)*, cat's tail *(Typha* spec.), bur reed *(Sparganium* spec.), etc. Especially the latter types are easy to maintain and can be planted in large baskets, without soil.

Due to their outstanding feature of depriving the fish's metabolic products from the water, plants should never lack in a pond in order to prevent an overdose of manure – resulting in a situation called eutrophia by the specialist. Of course some underwater plants would also be suitable, but their care requires too much effort in a garden pond. Only the hornwort, mentioned above, is an exception, because it grows no roots and floats freely in the water. As it extracts much of the overdose of nutrition, it should, like the above mentioned cat's tail and bur reed, including the swamp iris, not be absent in a pond, alone due to its cleansing effect.

As further decorations in an aquarium roots, stones, river gravel as well as bamboo canes can be used. However, you must be careful using the roots available in petshops, as they more or less strongly acidify the water by releasing humic acids. The fish can get ill through the strong reduction of the pH value. But if the roots were in a warmwater aquarium for some time before being used in the pond they cause no problem.

Almost natural looking replicas of roots, made of ceramics, are also available in shops which obviously are not problematic at all. For the creation of terraces, readymade ceramic pieces are available, which make the work much easier. By the way, if bamboo canes shall be used, then both their ends require to be sealed with liquid glass (sodium tetra-silicate), by dipping both ends into it and after drying them, repeating the procedure once again. Thus, no air can enter

through the open ends of the cane and cause it to turn black and rotten quickly. Sodium tetra-silicate is an unpoisonous, colourless liquid, which is available at the chemist.

It must however be kept in mind that through various materials the aquarium decoration should make a natural look and not turn tasteless. In some countries red, blue or green coloured gravel is commonly used to build up the ground. For plantation, shrill coloured plastic plants or artificial corals are used. Maybe among the fishes the little mermaid bubbles softly or a small UFO floats time and again, driven by air, up to the surface and sinks back to the bottom. This may be exciting for some children, and although the goldfish take it also quite cool, all this indeed has not much to do with nature.

3.4 Water Conditions

All types of goldfish require no special water conditions, including temperature, whether in an aquarium or a pond. Only the pH, i.e. the degree of "acidity" in water, appears to effect the goldfish mostly. Therefore, the pH value should be neutral, around seven, or slightly deviate above or below it. Although a pH value between 6 and 8 will be tolerated, the optimum seems to be around 6.7. Anyway, you should be careful when introducing the fish and moreover, should occasionally test the pH value of the water with a pH measure strip.

Water hardness appears to pose less of a problem for the goldfish and a total hardness between 10 and 15 degrees (resp. 180 to 270 ppm) seems ideal. In areas with extremely hard water the quality can be improved through the addition of soft spring water. The degree of hardness of the water in your water supply can be either tested and occasionally proofed by yourself, or asked at the local water works. Often, local aquarium clubs help and give advice, as well as they can test the water hardness and suggest the suitable spring sources in the vicinity.

Rain water is problematic, due to the density of pollutants, not only in the heavily populated areas. But, if you are able to catch the rain water after the first shower, then it can certainly be considered for use. Adding

Goldfish and Their Care
Goldfish as Community Fish

some water care products like Amtra Care, AquaSafe, aquatan, DESA fin, Duplagan, etc. can absorbe various heavy metals as well as chlorine. The latter usually is absent in rain water. Also a short filtering over activated charcoal can improve the quality of the rain water collected. Rain water should never be allowed to flow directly from the roof into the pond.

Finally the goldfish also show great tolerance regarding water temperature. Although the fish is categorized as a cold water fish, the water temperature in its homeland is around 18 to 20°C. However, it accepts higher and lower temperatures without problem. You nevertheless should allow the fish, like all other fish types, to acclimatise to the changed temperature range. If the temperature difference is more than 5°C, then a step-by-step acclimatisation is advisable.

In our region, the goldfish can spend the winter in a garden pond without problems, even when the water surface is frozen. All the top quality goldfish, these are the squat types, which are generally termed as fancy goldfish by us, require, however, warmth and should not be kept in water temperatures below 10°C.

4. Goldfish and Their Care

4.1 Goldfish as Community Fish

The goldfish has a very peaceful nature and its association with other fish causes no problems. However, a few rules have to be paid attention to. Although keeping goldfish together with tropical fish would be possible, especially when keeping fancy goldfish, which require a higher temperature, but due to the very differing biotopes the fish originate from it should not be taken into consideration. Also goldfish as coldwater fish need a winter period with more or less lower water temperatures, most of all if you decide to breed.

It is also possible that the long finned high quality fish are persecuted by the tropical ones and sooner or later become ill. Although goldfish very seldom terrorize other fish, it is nevertheless possible that small fish are seen as food or that the female

is annoyed during the mating season. As in my aquariums already two times a young fish lost an eye, while I was keeping it together with three adult lion-heads, I cannot recommend to keep together fish with very different size in one aquarium. In this case I presume the young fish lost their eyes as they tried to eat too eagerly.

As the goldfish is a slow and a peaceful inhabitant of our pond and aquarium, it often is discriminated against other fish during feeding. Therefore, you should not necessarily keep the quick and very active orfe or golden orfe together with the simple goldfish, Comet or Shubunkin. Otherwise, at feeding time, everything is already finished before the phlegmatic goldfish notice that it is lunchtime.

In an aquarium, attention must be paid to a similar problem between different varieties of fancy goldfish. Fish with extraordinary long veiltype fins have a disadvantage compared to the short tailed and thus quicker types. This is especially valid for the fishes with changed forms of eyes, like the dragon-eyes, celestials or bubble-eyes. These types of fish discover their food mainly through its smell. Therefore they hang on the surface shortly after the food has been dropped in and gulp in everything with the hope of eventually getting some food along with it. After a short period, they search the bottom for the sunk morsels. But only accidentally they pick up pieces floating in the water.

The problem of the goldfish with narial bouquets is a little different. Other types of fish in the same tank could be tempted to consider the plush-balls as food and possibly tear them of. Its association with the dragon-eye and similar types is hence advisable. In this case the pompons are secure, due to the dragon-eyes' reduced vision, however, now the fish with pompons have an advantage during feeding, provided its view is not restricted due to very large pompoms.

In the high-headed types the eyes can partially be covered by the head growth, leading to a reduced vision, like that of the dragon-eye, bubble-eye and the celestial, and may be a disadvantage during the feeding. Therefore, their association with the quicker types, like the Ryukin, etc., is not advisable, which quickly snap away the food before their mouths.

left: Two ironcoloured lion-heads with fringtail.

right: Very nice orange coloured bubble-eyes, the one on the left due to its well rounded form easily being recognized as a female.
Photos: B. Kahl

The fish with bubble-eyes are not just a little bit helpless and disadvantaged while feeding, in the course of which they search for food mostly on the ground, but also are endangered due to the form of their eyes themselves. Therefore, apart from the round pebbles no other type of stones should be used for decoration purposes.

Especially sharp edged gravel should be avoided, since fish with bubble-eyes are

below: View into a goldfish shop in Hong Kong; at the lower row in the second aquarium from the right: Red and white Dragoneyes, then butterfly tails, in all other aquariums top quality Ranchus.
Photo: A. Lim

Goldfish and Their Care
The Feeding

found very often on the ground, especially while searching for their food, and could injure themselves. Attention must also be paid that strong filters do not suck up their eye sacks and injure them. The injured bubbles could leak out and will not be regenerated. This type of fish should also never be caught with a net, but with the help of a little bowl. It should hence be transferred with the water in the bowl into the new aquarium and set in carefully.

A threefold coloured lion-head (Oranda) with fantail of excellent quality. Photo: A. Lim

4.2 The Feeding

The goldfish, which belongs to the carp fishes, is omnivorous. In its diet vegetable parts form the majority. This does not naturally mean that you can feed them everything. The fish need a varied, balanced diet with plenty of carbohydrates. This is especially important for the more or less squated fancy goldfish breeds, whose digestive organs are displaced and squeezed due to its body form.

Goldfish have an enormous appetite and always swim hungry through the water looking out for food. The fish once acclimatized to the aquarium immediately come to the front glass as soon as you enter the room, and then wait just below the water surface, hoping for food. On the contrary, they do not have a very large stomach and hence cannot take in large amounts of food. This must be considered while feeding. Overfeeding has to be avoided for two reasons, first from the point of health, and second, to minimize the water pollution.

Therefore, you should never feed more than will be eaten easily in ten minutes. If possible, you should feed twice or even three times a day in small portions. But, again, overfeeding must be avoided absolutely. Goldfish more often die due to fat-liver caused by overfeeding than starving.

During the summer time, you should, without hezitation, plan one fasting day per week, or you may easily leave the fish

A natural biotop with its luxurious growth of marsh marigold, waterlilies, spear-leaves, lilies, etc. at the Hottonia e.V., Darmstadt's aquarium club. In such a rich plantation goldfish can live, but will never be seen again. Photo: P. Sicka

without food for a weekend if you are not at home. If the water temperature sinks below 15°C, the metabolic processes of the fish become reduced and hence not too much food will be eaten, which must be paid attention to when feeding. If the fish is kept in the pond the whole year, the feeding should be stopped already at a water temperature around 8 – 10°C, as no food will be digested at this temperature. With a little experience, you should notice soon by the behaviour of the fish when the feeding needs to be stopped. Then the fish swim very slowly and hesitating to the food source and also show not much appetite.

Now to the food itself. There are various types of food available in the petshops. Among them you'll foremost find the flake food, sticks or pellets, deep-frozen and freeze-dried food, as well as to some extent also live food. Most of the big petfood manufacturers have special mixtures for pondfish and even for goldfish.

Flakes are the ideal form of food for all types of goldfish, up to medium size. They float on the surface, get quickly soaked and soft and hence are easier to digest. The manufacturers have flakes in several different varieties, as well as flakes with a higher portion of vegetable ingredients.

The larger fish should, however, be fed with smaller pellets and/or sticks. The pellets float on the surface or sink down gradually, but do not break into pieces and thus do not pollute the water. Both the pellets and the sticks are available in different compositions. Ideally, they contain raw proteins, lysin, raw fibre, unrefined fats and raw ash. Some of the sortiment is even completed with vitamins or Spirulina.

Japanese goldfish and Koi pellets are also available in the shops. Koi pellets are usually sold in three different granulations, in case the special goldfish pellets are not available. The small and medium types of the Koi-pellets are also suitable for the goldfish and make an excellent food. Pellets with Spirulina, a type of algae containing carotine, especially enhances a strong red colour in the fish. By now, Koi pellets are produced by the domestic food producers.

All kinds of sticks and pellets must be softened in water between five to ten minutes before being fed. Dry pellets are difficult to digest and start swelling in the digestive tract. When swallowed in large numbers, they can cause severe digestive problems and swellings, especially in the fancy goldfish breeds of the squat type with its displaced or rather squeezed digestive organs.

Often such fish, usually always the same ones, can be seen floating at the surface, belly up, for hours or float up time and again while swimming. Mostly this is cured automatically next day. However, in more serious cases this can cause constipation and, more worse, may also cause the death of the fish.

Amongst the deep-frozen and freeze-dried food chiefly the bloodworms (the larvae of the Chironomus mosquito), white and black mosquito larvae, daphniae, brine shrimps and Tubifex worms have to be considered. Additionally the deep frozen brine shrimps are recommendable, which are very important for the raising of young fish. All these types of food are available from time to time as live food or can be bred or caught by yourself.

When feeding live food attention has to be paid that it is thoroughly washed beforehand, in order to avoid the introduction of infections and diseases into the aquarium. This does especially apply the all-season available Tubifex worms, which preferrably live in extremely polluted waters. In China, they are grown in large ponds, whose grounds are first covered with chicken dung, and from which the Tubifex are literally harvested.

In China Tubifex worms, beside the bloodworms, are a much preferred food for the conditioning of the goldfish. While bloodworms as food are appreciated for a quick increase in the body mass of the goldfish, Tubifex are especially fed to the high-headed types, since the head growings get enhanced even more this way.

As fresh plant diet have to be considered, too, all duckweeds, coarsely chopped deep frozen spinach and deep frozen greenpeas, along with the plantation in the aquarium. The peas, however, have to be cleaned from the thin skin covering, so that they can be eaten more easily.

The owners of warm water aquariums can put the parts of the plants or whole plants left after the usual thinning out into the goldfish tank or pond and see what is eaten eventually. The same is with pond plants, with the goldfisch preferring also Rorippa beside the various duckweeds.

Moreover, in the Chinese literature on the keeping of goldfish an occasional feeding of minced pig- or cow-heart, pig-liver or fish-fillet is also advised. It is easy to freeze into small portions and thus is ever ready at hand. It is, however, not much preferred by the goldfish and also not easily digested.

The goldfish pudding, a gelatine food, is much better and similarly preservable, but unfortunately not available in the shops. However, you can prepare it easily yourself by cooking whole meat flour, fishmeal, eggs, vegetables and vitamins together and finally adding gelatine to thicken it. This kind of goldfish pudding is normally given as main-food in the huge fish farms.

Also the use of the leaves of young Chinese cabbage is advised and should be taken into consideration. This can be kept for some time in the refrigerator and hence is easily accessible. For the feeding, the mid-rib is cut out and the young leaves are cut into thin strips and then fed.

The Chinese fish breeders especially prefer the duckweed and the blood worms, because both of them result in intensive coloration of the goldfish, while the blood worms cause a quick increase in weight, on top of it.

4.3 The Technics

Apart from the aquarium for our goldfish, we require also a little bit of technics for its filtration, lighting and airation, without which an aquarium hardly can function. Although all three points could be quickly explained, it is nevertheless important to first understand the chemical processes that take place in the water, in order to better understand the demands of the technology. Hereafter we can return to our goldfish. Whoever is more interested in this matter may look in one of the various books on aquarium technics and water chemistry offered by the specialized trade.

The function of the filter is to remove all the undesirable rests of the metabolic processes of our fishes, the rotting leaves of the plants, and the uneaten food. This waste products consist of proteins to a large extant, which contain relatively much nitrogen. This nitrogen, bound organically in the aminoacids, in the water changes into inorganic ammonium through an oxidational process.

Even though ammonium in normal concentrations isn't poisonous for the fish, it may change rapidly into ammonia, which is poisonous. With an increasing pH value of the water the percentage of the poisonous ammonia also increases, which however changes back to ammonium with the decrease of the pH value. Hence, with a sudden increase of the pH value, for instance, through the partial change of water with alkaline water or due to a reduction of carbon dioxide contents the ammonia concentration can increase, with the result that sudden deaths of some fish may occur due to the ammonia poisoning, without any visible causes for their deaths.

Nevertheless, ammonium is a valuable source of nitrogen for the aquarium plantation and is reduced by them to a certain extent. In the normal aquarium, however, the proportion of fish to plants is far too high, so that not all of the ammonium can be removed. The overdose of ammonium can yet be changed through oxidization in a bacterial process, called denitrification, through the next stage of the poisonous nitrate into the relatively harmless nitrate. This nitrogen reduction takes chiefly place in the filter of our aquarium.

As a too high concentration of nitrate in our drinking water is undesirable, you wonder what happens to the ever increasing nitrate concentration. Well, for one thing, it serves as fertiliser for the plants, and secondly, it can be removed through bacterial reduction or partial water change. The plants have to change the nitrate through a complex process, with the help of iron, back into ammonium, before they can use it. Therefore they prefer the ammonium dissolved in water as a nitrogen source.

Also the bacterial reduction, in the course of which nitrate is reduced into nitrogen gas, is difficult, as it can take place only in an anaerobic, i.e. in an oxygen free milieu. This can be produced in an additional filter, which runs very slowly with only part of the water of the first filtration stage. This filter must, however, be fed from time to time with a fluid nutrient for the bacterial culture in order

left: Very nice big Panda lion-head with white headgrowth. Photo: K.-H. Bernhardt

right: On the right a redcaped fring tail, in China also called redcrowned crane. Photo: F. Teigler, A.C.S.

below: Red and black tigerhead with butterfly tail. In China this coloration is called "gold wrapped in iron". The light coloured spot on the head is called jade-seal. Photo: B. Teichfischer

to keep it alive. If the aquarium gravel has a certain height, the formation of an anaerobic milieu in some gaps is possible, where the bacteria can settle and contribute, even in a comparatively small way, to the reduction of the nitrate.

Due to the danger of poisoning by too high ammonia and nitrite concentrations, you should check these parameters on a regular base. In the petshops different test kits or measure strips are available, which make it easier for the unexperienced to check the concentration of these ingredients. As approximate value we consider a continuous concentration of 0.02 mg/l ammonia and 0.5 mg/l nitrite as already in question to keep our fish healthy, if it's not already harmful for the fish.

If the required type of bacteria of the genera Nitrosomonas and Nitrobacter are absent in newly set-up aquariums or the filter material, the concentration of poisonous nitrite or ammonia can increase when putting in the fishes too early. After about three weeks enough bacteria have developed, the filter works and, therefore, the change of waste particles into the non-poisonous nitrate takes place rapidly now.

Also the usage of certain drugs or radical preparations for a destruction of algae can disturb the bacterial population in the filter, or even destroy it completely, which would result in similar problems.

This waiting time can be reduced a little by inoculating the filter or the aquarium water with bacteria. The easiest way is taking the old (unwashed) filter material from a different, longrunning filter and putting it into the new one, or by mixing a bought bacteria preparation with the water. Despite all these helpful methods, the time before the first fishes are set in should never be reduced too much. By no way it is possible to put the fish the very same day into the newly set up aquarium or within the first week.

Now let's stop discussing the chemical processes. There is plenty of literature available on this subject, including regular articles in the aquaristic journals, which deal specifically with this matter. As a conclusion of the above presented short description of the reduction of nitrogen compounds, which takes place through the absorption of ammonium and nitrate by the plants and their "absorption" by our goldfish in turn, thus completing the nitrogen cycle, the importance of a good filtration system and often partial water changes becomes apparent. Further reasons for the cleaned-up

Goldfish and Their Care
The Technics

keeping of the fish are explained below under fish diseases.

The filter should accordingly be sufficiently proportioned and filled with the proper materials, in order to take out the undesirable harmful substances from the water. But what does "sufficiently" mean? In petshops, various types of external filters are available, which are run by an electrical pump. The internal filters, mainly run by air from a membrane pump, are suitable only for small aquariums. Proportionate to the power of the pump the volume of an aquarium is calculated for which the filter is suitable. However, it is more advisable to take the next larger size of a filter, as then there is more space for the filter material. If the pressure of the water flowing through it is too strong, it can be reduced easily at the filter's outlet.

A special sponge, which is available with small or large pores, serves as the filter material, along with ceramic tubules and similar materials, in order to provide an as large as possible surface for the nitrate reducing bacteria. These ceramic tubules are filled between the big pored sponge at the filters inlet and the fine pored sponge on the outlet. It is obvious that the filter has to be washed quarterly or every half year, according to the amount of accumulated waste. Attention must be paid that part of

the filter material always has to be returned back into the filter without being thoroughly washed, thus not to completely wash out the bacterial cultures.

The filtration of the water of a garden pond is much more a problem, as with the larger water body we have to calculate with larger filters and larger pumps. Ideally you can use the socalled Vortex filters as prefilters, and joined to it some special filtration chambers with brushes or hair curlers. To equip a large pond filter with

A park in Su-zhou with a goldfish bowl on display. Behind it an artistically carved window giving view to a rocky scenery.

On the left the Wang-shi park in Su-zhou, well known for its fine architecture and its forest sceneries. Su-zhou, located at the old Grand Canal, is supposed to be the secondmost beautiful place in China after Hang-zhou. The city is renowed, beside the Han-shan si, the Frosty Mountain Monastery, foremost because of its lovely old parks, of which there are plenty. In such parks bonsai and goldfish are on exhibition quite often. Photos: K.-H. Bernhardt

ceramic tubules would be much too expensive.

The Vortex filter is a roundshaped plastic container which is sharply pointed towards its lower end and has an outlet with a ventile at its bottom. The water is streaming into the filter from the one side, where it's whirling in a cirle. During this process the larger dirt particles sink to the bottom where they are literally washed out. By an overflow on the upper surface of the filter the water runs into the next filter where the smaller particles are reduced.

Occasionally as a final filter sand filters from the professional swimming-pool technics are used, however, these need relatively strong pumps as well as larger water amounts to clean the filter by reverse flushing. Much more natural and as effective are also reed beds, with the water flowing through them and then back into the pond. However, they need a lot of space and a slight slope with the result that they can't be used everywhere.

Almost as important as the filtering is the partial change of water. Therewith not only the overdose of nitrate but also other undesirable residue is taken out of the water. Fresh water addition not only adds trace elements but also reduces the hardness of the aquarium water a little, which is gradually increased due to the evaporation of water.

Generally it is advised to renew one third of the aquarium water every month. However, it is far better for keeping a constant pH value, apart from being less effort, to change about 10% of the aquarium water weekly, which may then be easily used for the further watering of the plants in the house.

This "used water" is much better for indoor plants than the tap water, and adding fertiliser is no longer necessary. With the garden pond you do nearly the same as you take out the water with a diving pump and use it to water the green and let the tap water normally used for this purpose run into the pond.

As the plantation is also important for the reduction of harmful substances, provision of sufficient light is required. The day-light neon-tubes have proved here to be easiest and most unproblematic. Even though one neon-tube might be sufficient for a few plants, for a luxurious plantation and, especially for higher aquariums, two or even more tubes are required. Here you can mix the normal day-light tubes with those especially made for plant lighting.

Finally to mention the airation. Although in the modern aquarism one has departed from the good old bubbling airstone as a sufficient plantation normally provides enough oxygen, however, aquariums with large goldfish should not necessarily be without it. At least membrane pumps, tubes and airstones should be at hand in order to be able to react immediately in case problems with the respiration appear. In a goldfish aquarium, the plantation alone is not sufficient to provide the fish with enough oxygen.

4.4 Acclimatisation of the Fish

One of the most exciting moments in fish-keeping, apart from the setting-up of the aquarium, is certainly the time of purchase of the first fishes. And precisely this step requires a special preparation. As you do not wish to bring in diseases along with the new fish (for further information please see the chapter on illnesses), you should always have an aquarium ready to be used as a quarantine aquarium for the newly purchased fish.

Precisely due to this reason, one should never buy any fishes spontaneously, even when there is a special and attractive offer. But as (almost) all of us are aware that it is not always possible to keep away from such temptations, it's essential to keep an empty aquarium to be used as a temporary quarantine aquarium.

Through the transport the fish are extraordinary stressed and thus prone to all kinds of illnesses, whose germs are present in almost all aquarium waters. All newly bought fish should be kept for at least two weeks in quarantine, as this is the longest latent period of the most common fish diseases. Latent period is the time between the infection with the germ itself and the outbreak of the illness. Even when the fish appear to be completely healthy and you would love to see them in the large display aquarium along with the other pretty fish, the quarantine period should be paid full attention to.

Goldfish and Their Care
Through the Winter

In order to adjust the temperature, the plastic bag containing the newly bought fish should be left for about half an hour floating in the quarantine tank. As already mentioned above, the water in the transport bag, most probably having the quality of its previous aquarium water, should not be too different from that of the water in the quarantine tank, regarding its temperature and pH value.

If this is not the case, then the values have to be adjusted slowly or the time span of thirty minutes has to be increased. After about half the time is over, you should open the bag and put in some water from the new aquarium. While the fish remain in the bag, a few crumbs of potassium permanganate are put into the water, along with a few drops of methylene blue, in order to kill organisms like fungi, worms or ectoparasites. In this bath, which should additionally be airated, the fish should stay for about ten more minutes.

Hereafter, you gradually add some more water from the quarantine aquarium to the bag and eventually release the fish into the new tank, when the 30 minutes are over. The water of the transport bag should be thrown away to avoid to import unwanted germs into the aquarium. A few drops of malachite green or a similar medicine from the petshop are added now to the water of the quarantine aquarium in order to prevent ich and other skin parasites.

You can also add some salt into the water, which is a prophylactic method against diseases as well. A concentration of one gram to twelve litres water having a hardness of 12°dH (resp. ca. 215 ppm; according to Krause) is completely safe for the fish over a longer period. In harder water the concentration should be increased to 3 g per 10 litre of water. But for some plants, however, a concentration of 2 g/10 l is already damaging.

The temperature of the water in the quarantine aquarium should be at least 20°C, in order to enhance the effects of the medicine. If it's lower, then the temperature has to be increased in small steps, however, a temperature difference of more than 5°C should be avoided. If the fish has open wounds or is suffering from obvious bacterial diseases, Furamon from the petshop or tetracycline (200 mg/10 litre) should be added to the water for several days. If the newly bought fish have survived this drastic treatment, they obviously were 100% healthy, and now you can safely accompany it with the other fish.

4.5 Through the Winter

As already briefly mentioned above, all types of carplike breeding forms with normal caudal fin like the common goldfish, Comet and Shubunkin, can be left in the pond the whole year long, provided it is deep enough and the water does not freeze right to the bottom. The first quality breeds stay in the garden only for summer, anyway, and are returned to their quarters in autumn.

The depth of the water in the pond should measure at least one metre at the deepest point. There, the water temperature in winter is around 4°C, as the water at this temperature is heaviest, as we had to learn in the physics lesson during our school days. Colder water, resp. warmer water in summer, rises to the surface.

If the water surface freezes in winter, then an opening has to be provided to maintain the gas exchange. In former times you managed this with a very simple method by sticking a small bundle of straw through the ice surface. Today different types of equipments made out of styrofoam, which float on the waters surface and keep an ice-free opening are available at specialized dealers.

Also a floating filter or an airstone, which provide some current on the surface, can be of help, if the temperature is not too low. Under no circumstances the air stone should be placed within the deeper zone of the pond, as this would just transport the warmer water from near the bottom to the surface.

In the older literature you sometimes can read the suggestion to let some water run out of the pond, in order to have some air between the ice and the water. With this method the problem becomes only delayed but not solved, as now the various gases rising out of the pond cannot escape, but only accumulate between the surface and the ice and now hinder the gas exchange.

Under no circumstances you should try to make a hole in the ice with any tools. For one thing, the fish, receiving the vibration of the noise from their lateral line organs would be

Goldfish and Their Care
Diseases and Their Prevention

A very nice Calico Ryukin.
Photo: Mainland Tropical
Fish Farm

the high headed types, in order to prevent furunculosis.

4.6 Diseases and Their Prevention

There is plenty of literature available which specifically deals with fish diseases and their treatment. A good standard book is the one from Dieter Untergasser, which should be on every aquarist's book shelf. Further books related to this subject are mentioned in the literature list. Nevertheless, I would like to mention some of the often occuring diseases in goldfish, which should enable a first orientation in this matter.

Of course also for goldfish this rule is true: prevention is better than curing. Therefore, attention should always be paid to the good quality and cleanness of the water. Polluted water weakens the organism of the fish and is often a source of illness. A bad quality of water can, for instance, lead to turbidity of the fluid in the bubbles of the bubble-eyes and the bubbles can develop bloody spots. If they have turned turbid once, it's very difficult to undo this development.

Thus we often, at best daily, should watch the fish for some time, for example during and shortly after the feeding, as the illnesses are better curable when detected early and

jerked out of their hibernation break and hence require unnecessary energy, on the other hand, this could injure their air bladder. If a hole has to be made in the ice layer, then this always can be achieved easily with the help of hot water.

In late autumn, when the temperature sinks, the amount of food should be reduced. If the temperature is below 10°C, feeding should be stopped totally. The fish lives on its body reserves now which it had stocked up to now. The water temperature for the fancy goldfish forms, that spends the winter in the cellar or similar places, should always be kept above 10°C. This is especially important for

Very well formed Red and White Ryukin with nicely pronounced humps. The Ryukin was breed after 1680 in the Ryukyu Archipelago (jap. Ryukyu retto, that means Pearl Archipelago), of which the best known island is Okinawa. Originating from this formerly independent kingdom with good trade relations to China the Ryukin came to Japan; its name is the shortened form of Ryukyu Ginkyo (Ryukyu Goldfish).
Photo: H. J. Mayland

Goldfish and Their Care
Diseases and Their Prevention

treated immediately. Healthy fish go quickly for the food and feed voraciously. Mostly they are waiting already when the keeper enters the room.

An ill fish is lethargic and swims slowly or rests without movement under the water surface or lies on the ground. Also a wobbling movement or scraping at the settings in the aquarium or along the bottom, wide open scales, bloody areas of the skin as well as white or grey coverings on the skin are symptoms of disease.

This is also a fact when the goldfish is losing more and more weight despite good food intake. A further symptom are respirative problems, with the fish opening its mouth wide in order to breath, or its gill covers spread wide open. However, this can also be a sign of a low oxygen content, when the pond is exposed quite long to intensive sunshine.

Another method of prevention is the above mentioned quarantine, which should be paid attention to. It happens even to the experienced aquarists from time to time, that by introducing some apparently healthy fish which came across by chance in a sale's offer

An orange veiltail with white lips and white caudal fins, you can see the extremely elongated pelvic fins very well. Photo: K.-H. Bernhardt

or were obtained cheaply from an acquaintance, diseases were brought to your own collection of fish, because there was no quarantine aquarium at hand for the newly acquired fish.

Orange and orangewhite celestials. The eyeballs of fish with a light colouring often look bluish. Photo: H. J. Mayland

Therefore, the purchase of the fish should always be planned and prepared. But the fish itself does not necessarily need to have been ill already. The transport itself could stress it so much as well as the new companions in the new aquarium, which perhaps do not keep the peace, that it can result in the outbreak of a latent illness or give the germs always present in every aquarium the chance for an attack.

Just imagine all the distance the fish have travelled to get here. In the country of their origin, let it be China, Hong Kong, Japan, or Singapore, they were caught in the large fish breeding farms and then sorted. Then, they maybe were packed and transported to an auction where they were sold, repacked and then transported by aeroplane over thousands of kilometers to Europa or America where they become unpacked again. Then they were kept there for a shorter or longer period, until they were caught and packed again to be transported to the local petshop, just another stopover on the long journey to their final domicile. Quite stressy, or don't you think so, especially if you consider that often some sedatives or narcotics are added to the water for the long flight.

A healthy fish kept in clean water is less prone to any disease and tolerates changes in temperature more easily. If the fish are weakened and/or exposed to stress, through hibernation or due to transport, they are more prone to the various illnesses.

But now let us have a look at the diseases themselves. Beginners with little experience might have difficulties to recognize an illness in time and even more to diagnose it correctly. Since veterinarians often can not help either, in case of any doubt you should consult some persons keeping fish her/himself or you should get in touch with some helpful people from a local aquarium hobbyist club.

Since some time various treatments are available which can be used to treat several diseases, like Clont, Furamor-p, or Gold Oomed. The latter is especially adapted for cold water fish. However, a direct treatment of the illness is always preferred.

In general we are dealing with several causative organisms, like virusses, bacteria, protozoa, fungi, worms and external parasites. In this order the most common

diseases will be described hereafter. Another possibility could be internal or external tumors. The treatment should always take place in a separate hospital tank if not all inhabitants of the aquarium became ill. Additionally, you can always give preventive medicine into the primary aquarium.

As a good remedy which can be used for various diseases in goldfish and Kois normal cooking salt can be used. It is applied prophylactic or with little infected fish as a longterm bath in the primary tank (1 g for 12 litres in water of 12°dH (215 ppm), in harder water up to a maximum of 3 g on 10 litre) or as shortterm bath for 10 to 45 minutes in a separate tank (15 to 20 g salt per litre; both according to UNTERGASSER). During such a short bath the fish should be checked from time to time, in order to be able to interrupt the treatment in case of problems.

Generally you can say that smaller and weaker goldfish should be treated with a weaker dose of remedy at a higher temperature and for a shorter period of time, while the larger and stronger fish may be treated with a slightly larger dose at lower water temperatures and for a longer period. For all kinds of remedy, the directions given by the producer should be read carefully and should be dosed accordingly.

Bacterial Fin Rot
(Bacteriosus pinnarum)

The bacterial fin rot, shortly called **fin rot,** is caused by various bacteria of the species *Aeromonas, Pseudomonas* and *Vibrio*. It is caused mainly by bad keeping conditions. The fin rot is infectious and should be treated immediately.

In its early stage the disease is easily overlooked, as the edges of the fins, especially those of the caudal fin, are only slightly dull. Later the edges turn white and the fins get more and more split as the tissue between the fin rays decomposes. The fins get noticably smaller and smaller. The fin rot can also start from the caudal peduncle and spread from there towards the fin lobes.

As a treatment in not too severe cases it is often sufficient to transfer the fish into a tank with fresh aquarium water, whereupon the illness appears to fade away and the fins begin to recreate gradually. A substance sold at the chemists under the names of

Goldfish and Their Care
Diseases and Their Prevention

acriflavine or trypaflavine can be used. As preventional treatment (according to UNTERGASSER) you take 1 mg per litre water, for treatment in the early stages 3 mg per litre water and in severe cases the fish are treated in a special hospital tank with 5 mg/litre water. Also baths with nitrofurantoin can be given for over 15 days, with one medicine capsule being dissolved in 30 to 40 litres of water (UNTERGASSER).

Antibiotics, such as tetracycline or sulfonamide, are also effective, but require a veterinary's prescription. Available in petshops are remedies based upon alcalic brilliant-green, as Baktopur, Furamor-p, General Tonic, etc.

Furunculosis
(Erythrodermatitis)

Various bacteria of the species *Aeromonas* cause furunculosis. The illness appears in the form of abcesses and sores, 2–20 mm large, which later burst open and form open, bloody wounds. Later on these wounds various fungi appear as a secondary infection.

The treatment with sulfonamides or antibiotics is similar as described for dropsy. In slighter cases, these areas get healed by the beginning of spring or disappear at a better water quality. These slight cases occur very often during the winter time in the high-headed types of fancy goldfish, most of all in those with head growth, when the water temperature sinks below 10°C. The illness appears in the form of yellowish-white pustules on the head growth. If these pustules are opened, a purulent fluid flows out. An improvement of the water quality and an increase of temperature makes them disappear again.

Dropsy

Dropsy itself is actually no disease, but an accompanieing appearance of various bacterial diseases, like ***abdominal dropsy*** and ***fish tuberculosis.*** Both diseases are very infectious and often end with the death of the ill fish. As the germs normally are always present in the water, the cause are again the bad keeping conditions. Also, weak fish are more prone to become infected than a healthy and strong fish.

The abdominal dropsy, which has been intensively examined in the carps, to which the goldfish belongs, is spread through virusses, but bacteria are also participating. In the due course, large amounts of body liquid gather in the abdominal cavity. Through the collection of liquid the fish appears bloated and the scales stand from the body, similar to an open fir-cone. This reminds the normal appearance of pearl-scaled goldfish, whose scales seem to be standing from the body due to the deposits of calcium carbonate. For this reason the perlscale types of goldfish are not very much appreciated in the western countries.

Apart from this bloated appearance the eyes can also be protruding (exophthalmus). These protruding eyes should, however, not be mixed with the normal dragon-eyed goldfish. The affected fish often lays on the ground or hangs wobbling under the water surface and mostly shows no escape reflex.

A successful treatment is possible only at an early stage. The affected fish should be isolated immediately. They have to be transferred into a quarantine or hospital tank and treated there with Furanol. A treatment with antibiotics like tetracycline hydrochloride, chlor-tetracycline and oxy-tetracycline or with sulfonamides is also recommended. All these preparations require the veterinary's prescription and advice.

In petshops you can purchase Cyprinopur for a preventive treatment and the quite effective Furamon is also available. In China, at the first appearance of the illness they bath fish the for five to ten minutes at 10°C in a solution of 2% cooking salt and 3% sodium bi-carbonate (according to LI ZHEN).

The fish-tuberculosis has the same symptoms like the abdominal dropsy. However, the fish also can loose weight and then show a knife-shaped dorsal line. In addition, the colour often becomes pale. The illness usually drags along and one or the other fish dies every few months, now and then. It can also happen that the whole collection is lost in a short time. A treatment is not possible, and the effected fish should be isolated immediately and euthanized. Although tetracycline provides a shorttime success, mostly the illness breaks out again later. Hence, the focus should be on the preventive methods, like healthy food and good keeping conditions.

Goldfish and Their Care
Diseases and Their Prevention

Two red and white crowned pearlscales with fringetail. Note the elongated caudal fin, which is unfortunately bent towards one side. The headgrowth looks similar to two blisters. In Japan this form is called Hamanishiki, a relatively recently developed variety from the city of Hamamatsu, thus its name "Hama-Brocade"
Photo: H. J. Mayland

Ich
(Ichthyophthiriasis)

The most common illness appearing in the fish is the **white-dots disease**, which is also termed **Ichthyo** or shortly **Ich** or **Ick** as to be found in the name of some remedies. The pathogen of this illness is the ciliate *Ichthyophthirius multifiliis*. The infected fish shows a gradual spread of small white dots over the whole body.

For this disease there are plenty of remedies available and therefore it is quite easy to treat. The chances of recovery are accordingly quite high. When infected a bit, that means at the early stage of the disease, it is possible to treat it by slightly increasing the water temperature about two or three degrees. This increased temperature should also be kept when using any remedy. As Ich spreads easily, all the inhabitants of the aquarium should be included in the treatment.

Various preparations for the treatment are available at the pet-shops, e.g., Contralck, Costapur, Exrapid, Furamor-p, Faunamor-p, amongst others. The basic substance in most of the available Ich remedies is malachite green oxalate, which can be obtained at the chemist as well. It is, however, a skin irritant and moreover carcinogen and poisonous, if swallowed. Therefore, it is advisable to restrict to the remedy available in the specialized petshops.

On the right Calico pearlscales, viewed from the top the roundish form can be observed very well, which does not look similar to dropsy, a kind of disease. Typical also the relatively small webbed caudal fin and the slightly developed headgrowth.
Photo: B. Teichfischer

Slimy and Dull Skin
(Costiosis, Chilodonellosis)

The **slimy skin disease** is the most common and recurrent illness among goldfish. It mostly occurs at the end of autumn or at the end of winter and is supported by bad keeping conditions, as is the case in all the other illnesses as well.

Its cause are the various types of unicellular animals. One of them is **Costia necatrix**, a skin-flagellate (protozoon), i.e. a very tiny flagellate. Another one is *Chilodonella cyprini*, a heart-shaped and relatively large ciliate, at least compared with the former parasite. Also other ciliates apart from *Costia necatrix* like *Trichodina* sp. or *Tetrahymena pyriformis* are also found at the affected areas which embed themselves in the skin and feed on bacteria.

In case of being affected by *Costia*, dull areas appear on the skin, which can drop off when severely affected, and bloody spots appear at such places. When affected by *Chilodonella*, at first dull, then white, transparent looking patches appear, which have a clear circular or elliptical form and begin to coagulate. Also at these spots the skin peals off later. *Chilodonella* prefers mostly to settle in the region from the back of the head down to the dorsal fin, but it can be found in the gills, too.

The treatment for not too severe cases is a short bath from 10 to 45 minutes with cooking salt. In case of Costia, an increase in temperature to over 30°C is also helpful, as the flagellates die at that temperature.

Goldfish and Their Care
Diseases and Their Prevention

For medical purposes, remedies based on chemicals like alkaline brilliant-green, copper-sulphate or methylene blue, e.g. Costapur, Ektozon, FungiStop, Furamor-p, Mycopur, Omnisan, Punktol, etc. are advisable, and baths in such preparations are preferrable, as the first two substances are poisonous. Chilodonella and other ciliates, in severe case, are treated with remedies based on malachite green or methylene blue.

Skin Fungus
(Dermatomycosis)

Another, often occuring illness is the infection through various kinds of fungi, which cause mycosis. This disease is also called **fish-mould**. The infectors are the mucedine/hypomycetes (fungi) of the species *Saprolegnia*, *Achlya* and *Dictyuchus*. These fungi are present in every aquarium water and live on dead organic substances. They attack the fish when its natural resistance is diminished due to the lack of healthy mucous membrane.

The cause for this can be a mechanical injury of the skin and the mucous membrane by a net, torn out scales or bites. Also the mucous membrane may change due to abrupt changes of pH value, water hardness, temperature, etc. This can be caused by e.g. transferring the fish to a different tank or by addition of large amounts of rainwater. Also, the existing damages due to wounds or fin rot may offer a surface for the fungus to attack.

The effected spots of the fish have a white, cotton-wool type of film, which is visible with the normal eye. If the disease is not recognized and treated immediately, this film/coating spreads, until, in the advanced stage, the fungus enters the body tissue and the fish cannot be rescued anymore.

This illness occurs among goldfish mostly during the spring and, very seldom, during the rest of the year. In case of minimum infections, an increase in water temperature and the improvement of water quality is of help here as well.

For the treatment, short baths with cooking salt or potassium permanganate (1 g in 100 litre water; UNTERGASSER) as well as in

above: View of a "small" Japanese miniature garden with rocks, waterfall, and a pond in the form of a creek with Kois and a traditionally arched bridge at a house in Kyoto, the old Japanese imperial city.

left: Bamboo with stone lantern in the Hokuji monastery at Kamakura.

Lily at artificial waters in Japan.
Photos: K.-H. Bernhardt

severe cases a longer treatment with malachite green oxalate, as mentioned above, are recommended. However, there is plenty of remedy available in the petshops, which should be given preference. Worth mentioning are FungiStop, Furamor-p, Mycopur, Omnisan, etc. Among the preventive remedies Ectopur has to be named, for instance, and for the pond use DesaFin.

Gill Rot
(Branchiomycosis)

The *gill rot* appears mostly among fish kept in polluted water and especially in ponds during the summer. It is caused by the algal fungi of the genus *Branchiomyces,* which become embedded in the gills and cause the necrosis of the infected tissue.

The affected fish have great breathing problems and hang below the water surface gasping for air. They show no appetite and soon stop eating at all. A careful lifting of the gill covers, with a blunt object, will show, apart from the red and healthy gill lamella, also some white and necrotic tissue.

The same symptoms are visible in the bacterial gill rot and the gill necrosis, which can be caused by an extreme rise in the pH value during the increase of algae in the garden pond at spring time. An exact diagnosis is not possible for the unexperienced.

The treatment again is with cooking salt in a shortterm bath. Also remedies with alkaline brilliant-green may be used.

Parasites

The various types of trematode worms or flukes, fish leeches and copepod crustaceans, like the fish lice and anchor worms, belong to the external parasites. Amongst the various types of worms living parasitically there are, however, many that attack the internal organs and hence are not counted to the ectoparasites. Moreover, a proof is difficult for an amateur, as many of them are visible and thus determinable only with the microscope.

On imported fish, which were bred in large ponds on the fish farms, we sometimes find anchor worms *(Lernaea carassii),* an elongated, rounded crustacean. A quick breathing, but more so, the widespread opercula point to an infection with gill flukes. Hook-worms of the genera Dactylogyrus, Monocoelium, and Gyrodactylus, which parasite on the skin and gills of the fish, are the cause of this illness.

All these types of parasites luckily are very rare. Leech and fish lice may also be imported through self caught live food, which has not been put through a suitable sieve. Its treatment is by short baths in cooking salt, formaline (poisonous! 2–4ml of a 35–40% solution in 10 litre, bath for 30 min; UNTERGASSER) or with remedies like Clont, Ectopur, Formalite, Gurotox, Mycopur, etc., available at the petshop. If the anchor worms are not attached to deep with their anchorlike hooks, they may be pulled out gently with tweezers.

Capsize Disease

The capsize disease is not an illness in the sense of the word but a phenomenon which may occure at times with newly bought goldfish and which is described in the Japanese literature on goldfish under this name. The capsize disease manifests itself, as you would suppose from its name, in a way that fish, which were swimming perfectly in the tank of the trader before you purchased them, now topple over and swim belly up after they have been set in the new tank. Often they sink down to the ground in this position. After some time they return to their normal swimming position under difficulties, only to capsize again shortly afterwards.

This phenomenon shows up mostly among the high headed types of fancy goldfish and is caused by too great differences in water temperature when being transferred to the new tank. Often this is the result of not following the procedure as described in the section on acclimatisation or by transferring the fish to another tank in which the water temperature differs for more than 5°C from the first tank. Increasing the temperature for several days usually cures this problem.

Breeding
Goldfish Genetics

5. Breeding

Two of the, in my opinion, three large occasions in fish keeping have been mentioned above already. They are the setting up of an aquarium, where the very first one has its own special effect, and the purchasing of the fish. The third large occasion for every fish fancier is the time of breeding of her/his fish, to which attention shall be paid now.

The successful reproduction of the aquarium or terrarium animals is accompanied by a certain sense of satisfaction for the hobbyist, as this is a proof for optimal keeping conditions. The rearing of these young animals is another challenge for the keeper and offers multiple experiences. Commercial aspects are mostly only in the background. It is, however, also possible to simply enjoy the beautiful animals, without bothering the trouble of breeding.

5.1 Goldfish Genetics

Since more than thousand years the goldfish is kept by men and is bred and reproduced by him. As the goldfish is prone to mutations, these are natural changes in the genes, which have occured and still take place today, it was easy to aim at certain characters through selection and selective breeding, and to reproduce them furtheron through crossbreeding. Thus, over 300 different varieties have been produced until today, and still more new ones are added.

In China the hereditary transmission in the goldfish is now being researched more and more scientifically and the results are used increasingly in the breeding of new varieties. This is, however, not the theme of this small booklet. In this chapter attention shall be paid only to the reproduction and rearing of our goldfish. Detailed information on genetics in goldfish can be found in Smartt & Bundell.

It has its reasons that in goldfish we speak of varieties and not of races as in dogs, poultry, etc. Among the progeny of a certain variety there are always fish included which do not carry the special characters of their parents.

Even among the common goldfish not all the offspring have the reddish golden coloration, but among others they show grey to blackish colours as well. Although today the different Japanese strains of the Ranchu, which have been bred very selectively over many decades, now breed more purely than the other varieties, even here the progeny is not 100% pure genetically.

5.2 Spawning

Now to the breeding itself. If the goldfish have been fed enough on a protein rich diet during autumn and spring and have been kept in cool temperatures through the winter, then, with a considerable increase in temperature during late spring, the spawning follows spontaneously, without using any special methods, provided both sexes of fish are kept together. More on this subject a little later.

The spawning event is announced a few days in advance, as the fish chase each other through the whole aquarium. But this can also take place when only female fish are kept, as the released eggs are eaten with preference. The successful spawning can however be noticed by the water appearing more or less milky the next morning. If there are plenty of fine plants like javamoss and hornwort, they shall be covered with thousands of eggs which must be transferred to another aquarium as soon as possible, because the parents would otherwise eat up their spawn.

It is, however, easier to put the fish into a separate aquarium for spawning purposes. This is done either in pairs or in small groups of one milter and two to three spawners, or two milters and three to four spawners. It's obvious that all the fish must be of the same variety and should be free of defects.

The water level in the spawning aquarium should be between 15 to 20 cm high with a water surface of about one square meter, for larger spawning groups even more. The favourable water temperature is around 20°C. To form a substrate for spawning, fine plants such as hornwort, javamoss or waterweed should be placed into this tank, also branches of conifers (fir, thuja, cypress, etc.) are suitable. In the shops, artificial

Breeding
The Sexual Differences

some of them stick on the glasses as well, where they can also develop, provided they do not get lumped together. After the parents have been removed, you should put some methylene blue (30 mg/l) into this water to prevent spawning mould and also airate the water slightly.

5.3 The Sexual Differences

If different varieties are bred together, it is surely desirable to put together the fish with the same characters for reproduction purposes, in order to obtain a large number of progeny of the same variety. Therefore it is important to recognize the sex of the fish. This is, however, not easy for an unexperienced observer, as a prominent sexual dimorphism is missing in the goldfish. Sexual dimophism means the description of the differently developed body form and coloration in different sexes.

left: A red and white fringetail with narial bouquet and curled opercula. Photo: H. J. Mayland

right: Brown fantail with narial bouquet with four deeply red pompons. Photo: B. Teichfischer

below: Brown fantail with narial bouquet with orangewhite pompons. Photo: B.Teichfischer

spawning ropes are also availabe nowadays, not looking too dissimilar to bottle brushes which are made out of plastic cord. The eggs stick on this material and develop. Before placing the substrate in the spawning aquarium, all of it should be bathed in potassium permanganate for desinfection.

While a spawner with a body length of ten or more centimeters can produce between 6,000 to 18,000 eggs, young fish at their first spawning after all spawn between 1,000 to 2,000 eggs, thus enough spawning substrate should be provided. On this substrate most of the very sticky and transparent eggs adhere, which have an average length of 1–1.5 mm. Part of the eggs certainly will drop down to the bottom, while

Generally you can say that the female fish's abdomen appears well rounded and larger than that of the male of the same variety, even outside the spawning period. The male fish are supposed to have stronger colours and longer fins than females of the same age and variety. The pectoral fins of the males mostly appear longer and stronger or at least the first fin ray in this fin is longer as well as stronger than that of the female. The latter instead has a slightly thicker and stronger first fin ray of the anal fin(s) than the male and the area between anal fin and anus is formed much softer. The male has a harder bulge that can be felt by touching the fish, extending from the base of the anal fin to the anus, which appears a little carinal together with the slightly protruding anus.

Breeding
Rearing

During the spawning period, the female appears even rounder than the male, while the latter develop white tubercles on the opercula and on the first ray of the pectoral fins, due to the influence of sexual hormones. In rare cases these tubercles may occur also on the head and just behind the opercula. Very rarely and only in very small numbers these tubercles can also appear on the female. The spontaneous releasing of milk or eggs after a slight pressure on the abdomen, often already seen when lifting the fish out of the water with the hand, will often be sufficient to ascertain its sex.

Much experience nevertheless is required to define the sex on the base of the form of the anus and sexual opening. This should always be undertaken with the help of a magnifying glass. The cloaca of the male is smaller and longish to ovalshaped, while that of the female is round and slightly protruding.

next two to four days on the glass or other decorations of the setting. During this period the yolk-sac is fed upon and no other food is taken. Not before the end of this period, when the larvae swim to the water surface and fill their swimming bladder with air, they can swim horizontally and we no longer speak of larvae but call them fry or alevin.

Due to their minuteness, the fry require very small food. An excellent food are the tiny rotifers and other infusoria which you easily can prepare through a straw or banana peel infusion. However, in the shops also fluid fry food is available, which is of very good quality.

Equally approved for centuries in China and Japan has the feeding of hard boiled egg yolk, which is pressed through the finest gauze, like that of the brine shrimp sieve, and then dissolved in the water. At this point

left: Male with white tubercles as shown during the mating season. Photo: K.-H. Bernhardt

rechts: Young white lion-heads or better lion-head eggfish in order to avoid confusion with the Oranda lion-head. In contrast to the Japanese Ranchu their caudal peduncle is straight. Photo F. Schäfer

below: Calico eggfish. Photo: B. Teichfischer

5.4 Rearing

If the water has a constant temperature of 20°C the fry begin to hatch after five days, while at higher temperatures this happens earlier. According to Japanese research, too low or too high temperatures – below 15°C and above 26°C – are unfavourable for the development. Goldfish hatched under these temperatures often show deformed fins and other anomalies.

The transparent larvae of the goldfish have a length between 3 and 6 mm after hatching and are attached vertically for the

extreme caution is required as the egg yolk detoriates very quickly, as well in the refrigerator as in an aquarium, and can hence endanger the whole fry. It is therefore especially important during rearing, to feed often enough, but never too much, and to provide a weak airation and filtration through a sponge filter.

After about one week the fry are able to eat freshly hatched brine shrimps, tiny daphniae as well as dust food. Especially suitable as food for the fry are the daphniae and baby brine shrimps, because this diet enhances growth and vitality already in the very early stage of goldfish growth. For a healthy growth of the fry it is also of great importance that the breeding container is cleaned carefully often and that it is not overcrowded. Generally there should not be more than 25 fish, up to a length of 2 cm, in 30 litre water, or a maximum of 6 fish with a length of more than 2 cm.

5.5 Selecting the Fry

The newly hatched larvae still do not show much similarity with their parents, neither in colour nor in the rudimentarily formed fins. Completely independent of the parents' colours the goldfish fry are almost colourless after hatching and show a tinge of grey. This becomes gradually darker, until the fish appear almost black after about one month. Another month later the colour on the abdomen becomes gradually lighter, and after a more or less long time period the final colour is attained. This colour change takes place through an enzymatic destruction of certain pigment cells.

After about 15 days, when the fry have attained a length of approximately one centimeter, the shape of the caudal fin becomes gradually visible. As there are always some fish with more or less distinctive characters of the wild type among the fry, the first selection of the fry takes place already after 30 days. The undesirable wild types grow much quicker than the rest of the fry and are superior to it. Therefore, all the fish with deformations, simple or irregular caudal fin, an undesirable form of the latter and all the wild types get sorted out. At this occasion, the rest of the fry can also be

selected according to its size for further rearing and prevention of eventually occuring cannibalism.

After about three or four months the young fish are selected for a second time, when the actual colour is obvious or the colour change has come almost to an end. The period for attaining the final colour is different in each variety. The red-metallic fish generally attain their colour between six to nine months of age. The multicoloured calico variety begins as first with the colour change but takes longest in attaining a stable coloration. In very few of the varieties the black coloration of the young fish is totally missing. This includes, apart from the albinos, the bronze fish, which as a young is yellowish.

The selection of the fish, which are kept for the further breeding, follows later, when all the desired characters are fully formed. Under favourable conditions the young fish can be mature after one year already, although normally the male fish attain this level in the second year and the female not before the third. Good keeping can, by the way, enable the fish to live up to thirty years.

6. The Purchase of the Fish

While purchasing goldfish a few things have to be paid attention to and according to the purpose the fish is bought for, either to be kept in a garden pond, a show aquarium or as a breeder fish, they have to fulfill different conditions.

First class fish, which fulfill all your demands regarding shape and colour are extremely seldom, as only a small percentage of the fry meets your ideas. Accordingly they are very valuable and rather expensive. Normally such fish remain in the fish farms for the further breeding and hardly reach the market.

But foremost, the fish must be healthy and active, literally like a fish in the water. Especially for the squated types with long finnage it is important that it swims elegantly and vigorously. Fish that move around abnormally and in an obtrusive way or which dart around in the container in a helpless mode you should not buy. When the fish stop moving they must be able to keep their

The Purchase of the Fish

balance and not turn headover or turn a summersault.

If no quarantine tank is available where the newly purchased fish can be kept in, which is basically not advisable, it is of outmost importance to pay special attention to their health. The fish should have no large injuries of the skin or fins and shall be free of parasites. Small wounds and minor injuries of the fins, which can occur accidentally due to the long transportation, heel quickly in otherwise healthy fish and hence are acceptable.

To estimate the health of the fish may be quite difficult for a still unexperienced keeper, but is is quite easy to recognize any external infestations through ectoparasites like fish lice (*Argulus* sp.) or anchor worms (*Lernaea* sp.). Although both of these parasites are mentioned often in the literature, they are rather scarcely found and many of us might find them only on the pictures in the literature on fish. Many of the illnesses, as far as early recogniced and diagnosed in time, are easy to treat with the corresponding remedies. Experienced keepers are capable of healing a fish in a quarantine tank easily and thus could obtain an ill fish, when it is a especially beautiful specimen and if its price is reasonable.

If the fish is bought for the garden pond, it should have a broad, strong coloured back, as it will be seen only from the top. The squat types with long finnage, the so-called high breed quality or fancy goldfish, should not be considered as occupants of the pond. As mentioned above, their keeping in large ceramic or plastic bowls in the open during the summer is certainly possible. From these containers the fish can be caught and transferred back easier to the aquarium in autumn, without much stress for the fish or the keeper, as by catching them in a deeper pond with plenty of water plants.

Fish which are destinated for the aquarium, should have a broad surface looking from the side as they will be seen mostly from there. Due to this aspects it is of course helpful when you are able to see the fish from the side or the top already at the trader.

As already mentioned, some small injuries of the fins are acceptable, as these heel quickly. However, you should pay attention to the shape of all the fins. The fin rays should be free of any nodules. The caudal fin should be unfolded, hanging or spread gracefully, its upper lobe bent slightly downwards. Fish with a straight or bent upwards upper lobe should be avoided. Among the varieties with doubled caudal fins, the upper lobes should be completely separated on the top edge and not grown together, as it is required for Tosakin or goldfish with the so-called pinched tail, especially when you want to use them for breeding.

The dorsal fin, if there is one at all, should be standing straight and be spread out towards the back. The anal fins should be developed in pairs and should be covered by the lower lobes of the caudal fin. If the fish is only for display and not for breeding, then the completely or partially grown together upper lobes of the caudal fin as well as a simple or even missing anal fin are fully acceptable.

Lion-heads and Ranchus sometimes have problems keeping their balance. Their head sinks downwards while not swimming, and while swimming it can happen that they tumble over. This may appear very amusing, but these are less quality fish, which you should not buy. Fish of quality lineages do not show these characters.

Both these types of goldfish should have broad and massive heads, in order to provide enough space for the warty caps. Here attention has to be paid that the eyes are not covered by the growth. The head for all the other varieties apart from the high-headed types like lion-heads and Ranchus with their typical headgrowth should have a triangular shape with a slightly pointed mouth. This form is also termed as "mouse head" by the Chinese.

If the fish have enlarged eyes like the dragon-eyes, bubble-eyes and the celestials, these should be symmetrically formed. The liquid in the sac-like growth of the bubble-eyes should not be dull, and in celestials the pupils should be at a horizontal line, both having the same inclination angle. In China, fish with a red ring around the eyeball are preferred. However, there are also fish with blue rings around the eyeballs. In the different forms of the Shubunkin black rings are desirable.

Among the offspring of Ranchus from time to time fish appear which developed a dorsal fin. Such fish are normally selected

The Purchase of the Fish

On the left orangewhite Ranchu. The fish on top with plenty of white, while the lower one has the red colour nicely restricted to the head. The dorsal line should always show a regular curving, obtrusive protuberances caused by rests of the dorsal fin are undesirable. The picture on the right shows a Ranchu in Calico colouring.
Photos: above B. Kahl, right H. J. Mayland

The Ranchu is the most favourable goldfish in Japan, where it is the king of goldfish. Note the strongly curved back, which should ideally form an angle of 45° with the caudal fin. Within Chinese breeds, which would better be called lion-head eggfishes, the caudal penduncle ist mostly straight. Moreover note the coloration of their caudal fins. In two fish it is unicoloured or rather colourless, in two other ones it shows a ring of deep red at the base.The type of coloration the fish at the right bottom is performing is called Sakuranishiki, which translates as Cherry(blossom)brocade.
Photo: H. J. Mayland

very early from the other fry, but if the fish have a well formed dorsal fin, they are surely as attractive as those without and very much comparable to the high-headed types like Oranda, lion-head or tigerhead.

If the goldfish show any narial bouquets, attention should be paid that the pompons are developed big, compact and symmetrically. If the pompons hang too loose, they get sucked in by feeding or breathing and then blown out again, or they can get stuck in the plants or the filter inlet.

Unicoloured fish should have a strong and deep colour. In fish with two or more colours these should not be pale and should have a good contrast. The colour pattern should be beautifully mixed and spread over the body, ideally forming a symmetrical pattern on both sides of the body.

Among the various types of Shubunkin and calico (penta-coloured) types with elongated fins, a matt squamation along with metallic scales are desirable. Yet, the metallic portion should not be too large. The basic colour should ideally be a pale blue, but today also fish are available with a the colour from bluish-white to almost white. Usually the whole body is covered by a black dotted or striped pattern, while larger red and/or orange spots are spread all over. Relatively seldom fish are found with the red colour limited to the head only and therefore these very much sought after.

ISBN: 3-931702-69-3

ISBN: 3-931702-41-3

ISBN: 3-931702-39-1

ISBN: 3-931702-34-0

ISBN: 3-931702-43-X

ISBN: 3-931702-53-7

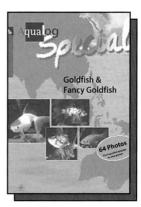

ISBN: 3-931702-45-6

ISBN: 3-931702-51-0

Upcoming specials:

Freshwater Coral Fish: Cichlids from Lake Tanganjika

The Colourful World of Livebearers

Decorative Aquaria : An Amazonas Biotope Tank

Decorative Aquaria : A Marine Tank for Beginners

Decorative Aquaria : A Dutch Waterplant Tank

Decorative Aquaria : Eastafrica Biotope Tank

Decorative Aquaria : Impressive Cichlids from Central America

Decorative Aquaria : Amazing Dwarf Cichlids from South America

Decorative Aquaria : An Aquaterrarium

Future Specials

Order your free copy of **AQUALOG***news* and the **AQUALOG** programme!

Infos and news:

AQUALOG Verlag GmbH
Liebigstr. 1
D-63110 Rodgau

Tel.: +49 (0) 06106 - 64 46 91
Fax: +49 (0) 06106 - 64 46 92

E-Mail: acs@aqualog.de
http://www.aqualog.de

The AQUALOG-System
Information and Description

AQUALOG Lexicon

The AQUALOG team has set itself the goal to catalogue all known ornamental fishes of the world – and this task will, of course, take several years, as there are over 40,000 fish species.

Compiling an AQUALOG lexicon, we take a certain group of fishes, label all known species with code-numbers, look for the newest results of fish research about natural distribution, features and maintenance of the fishes and try to get the best photographs, often from the most remote parts of the world.

Our ingenious code-number-system labels every species with its own individual code-number which the fish keeps even if a scientific re-naming occurs.

And not only the species gets a number, also each variety, distinguishing locality, colour, and breeding form.

This system makes every fish absolutely distinct for everybody. With it, international communication is very easy, because a simple number crosses almost all language barriers.

This is an advantage not only for dealers, but for hobbyists, too, and thus for all people involved in the aquarium hobby.

Again and again, new fish species are discovered or new varieties bred. Consequently, the number of fishes assigned to a certain group changes constantly and information from available specialist literature is only reliable within certain time limits. Thus, an identification lexicon that is up-to-date today is outdated after as little as one year.

To give aquarists an identification 'tool' that stays up-to-date for many years, we developed our ingenious patented code-number system.

When going to press, our books contain all fishes that are known to that date. All newly discovered or bred species are regularly published as either supplements or as so-called "stickups" in AQUALOG*news*.

These supplementary peel-back stickers can be attached to the empty pages in the back of the books.

As you can see, we provide the latest information from specialists for hobbyists. Over the years, your AQUALOG books will 'grow' to a complete encyclopaedia on ornamental fishes, a beautiful lexicon that is never outdated and easy to use.

AQUALOG*news*

AQUALOGnews is the first international newspaper for aquarists, published in four-colour print, available in either German or English language and full of the latest news from the aquatic world.

The following rubrics are included:Top Ten, Brand New, Evergreens, Technics, Terraristics, Fish Doctor and Flora. Further, there are travel accounts, breeding reports, stories about new and well-known fish etc.

The news gives us the opportunity to be highly actual, because up to one week before going to press, we can include reports and the 'hottest' available information.

This way, every six weeks a newspaper for friends of the aquarium hobby is published that makes sure to inform you about the latest 'arrivals' waiting for you at your local pet shop.

AQUALOG*news* can be subscribed to and contains 40 supplementary stickers for your AQUALOG books in 12 issues. You can subscribe to the news either via your local pet shop or directly at the publishers.

Issues without stickups (print run: 80,000) are available at well-sorted pet shops. The newspaper also informs you about newly published supplements.

AQUALOG Special

The Specials series is not intended to repeat all the things that were already known twenty years ago, like 'how to build your own aquarium' – something, probably nobody practises anymore, because there is no need to do so.

We provide the latest and most important information on fish keeping and tending in precise and easily understandable language.

We want to offer advice that helps you to avoid mistakes – and your fishes to live a healthy life.

We intend to win more and more friends for our beautiful and healthy (because stress-reducing!) hobby.

Order our new free catalogue, where all our previous and future books are shown and described.

Literature and Index (Poster)

Andrews, Dr. Chris; 1987. A Fishkeeper's Guide to Fancy Goldfishes. Blacksburg, VA

Baensch, Hans A. & Paffrath, Kurt & Seegers, Lothar. 1992. Gartenteich Atlas. Melle.ISBN 3-88244-024-4

Bassleer, G.; 1983. Bildatlas der Fischkrankheiten. Melsungen

David, Al; Garden Ponds, A Complete Introduction. Neptune, NJ

Franke, Wolfgang; 1990. Faszination Gartenteich. München. ISBN 3-405-13529-X

Geran, James; 1996. The Proper Care of Goldfish. Neptune, NJ

Ladiges, Prof. Dr. W.; . Coldwater Fish in the Home and Garden. Morris Plains, NJ

Ladiges, Prof. Dr. W.; . Kaltwasserfische. Melle

Li Zhen; 1990. Chinese Goldfisch. Peking, Morris Plains, NJ, ISBN 7-119-00408-5

Man Shek-Hay; 1993. Goldfish In Hong Kong. Hong Kong

Mertlich, Robert; 1995. Goldfisch, A Complete Guide. Neptune, NJ

Mertlich, Robert; 1995. Goldfish. A Complete Introduction. Neptune, NJ

Matsui, Dr. Yoshiichi & Axelrod, Dr. Herbert; 1991. Goldfish Guide. Neptune, NJ

Mayland, Hans J.; 1994. Goldfische und Farbkarpfen. Hannover. ISBN 3-7842-1108-9

Nitschke, Günther; 1991. Gartenarchitektur in Japan. Köln. ISBN 3-8228-0269-7

Ostrow, Marshall E.; 1985 + 1995. Goldfish. A Complete Pet Owner's Manual. Hong Kong

Pénzes, Bethen & Tölg, István; 1983. Goldfish and Ornamental Carp. New York.

Pénzes, Bethen & Tölg, István; 1983, 1993. Goldfische und Kois. Stuttgart. ISBN 3-8001-7215-1

Reichenbach-Klinke, H.-H.; 1968. Krankheiten der Aquarienfische. Stuttgart

ders.; 1975. Bestimmungsschlüssel zur Diagnose von Fischkrankheiten. Stuttgart

ders.; 1980. Krankheiten und Schädigungen der Fische. Stuttgart

Seike, Kiyoshi; Kudo, Masanobo & Schmidt, Walter; 1983. Japanische Gärten und Gartenteile. Stuttgart. ISBN 3-8001-6149-4

Sikora, Horst; 1980 Gartenteiche und Wasserspiele planen, anlegen und pflegen. Niedernhausen

Smartt, Joseph & Bundell, James H.; 1996. Goldfish Breeding and Genetics. Neptune, NJ. ISBN 0-7938-0090-0

Stadelmann, Peter; 1992, Der Bach im Garten. München. ISBN 3-7742-1077-2

Teichfischer, Bernhard. 1994. Goldfische in aller Welt. Melle. ISBN 3-89356-176-5

Untergasser, Dieter; 1989, Krankheiten der Aquarienfische. Stuttgart. ISBN 3-440-06048-9

Untergasser, Dieter & Axelrod, Herbert .; 1989, Handbook of Fish Diseases. Neptune, NJ. ISBN 0866227032

Ven, Jo in't. 1977, 1983. Goldfische und Farbkarpfen. Minden. ISBN 3-7907-0137-8

MAGAZINES:

AQUALOGnews
Verlag A.C.S. GmbH, ISSN 1430-9610

AQUARIUM FISH MAGAZINE
U.S.A.

AQUA PLAISIR
FRANCE, ISSN 1270-3813

ADDRESSES:

Texas Koi & Fancy Goldfish Society
http://www.texaskoi.org

Utah Koi and Fancy Goldfish Farm
http://www.cheek.com/~utahkoi

Koi- und Goldfisch Vet
http://www.koivet.com

The Goldfisch Society of America
http://www.geocities.com/Tokyo/4468/gfsa.html

Name	Code-No/Poster		Name	Code-No/Poster		Name	Code-No/Poster		Name	Code-No/Poster	
Aka Chotengan	X33445-3	B8	Fantail, red and white			Kuro shishigashira	X33518-6	F7	Ryukin, red		
Akademe(kin)	X33527-6	F3	with typical mousehead	X33414-5	B3	Kuro suihogan	X33309-6	H8	with slight Dragoneyes	X33527-6	F3
Akairo	X33500-5	B5	Fantail, red with white fin lobs	X33412-4	C3	Kurodeme (Kuro demekin)	X33384-4	A3	Ryukin, red-white	X33525-6	G3
Akairo Oranda	X33505-5	A5	Fringtail, blue	X33668-5	H2	Lan hu-tou	X33522-5	E6	San-hua gao-tou	X33510-4	D5
Akairo Tosakin	X33555-6	E4	GiniroTosakin	X33558-5	H4	Lan wen-yu	X33668-5	H2	San-hua hu-tou	X33523-5	F6
Akashiro Oranda	X33500-5	B5	Ginkyo (Hibuna)	X33055-5	A1	Lionhead, black (China Star)	X33518-6	F7	Sanshoku oranda shishigashira	X33510-4	D5
Akashiro Ranchu	X33601-5	B7	Goldfish, red and black	X33059-3	B1	Lionhead, claico (chinese Ranchu)	X33603-5	G7	Sanshoku oranda shishigashira	X33523-5	F6
Akashiro Ranchu	X33600-6	A7	Goldfish, red Dragoneyed	X33385-2	H1	Lionhead,			Sarasa Ryukin	X33525-6	G3
Akashiro	X33579-3	C4	Hanafusa	X33401-6	A8	red and black (Oranda)	X33520-5	C6	Sarasa suihogan	X33306-4	E8
Azumanishiki	X33435-4	H5	Hanafusa	X33413-4	G2	Lionhead, red caped			Seibun	X33668-5	H2
Bai shan-wei wen-yu	X33412-4	C3	He ding hong	X33411-5	E5	(chinese Ranchu)	X33517-3	E7	Shubunkin	X33059-3	B1
Bai shi-zi-tou	X33516-3	D7	Hei Long-jing	X33384-4	A3	Lionhead, red caped			Shubunkin	X33060-3	E1
Black Moor (Dragoneye)	X33384-4	A3	Hei shi-zi-tou	X33518-6	F7	(Red Crane-Crown)	X33411-5	E5	Shubunkin	X33096-4	F1
Bristol Shubunkin	X33096-4	F1	Hei shui-pao-yan	X33309-6	H8	Lionhead, white (chinese Ranchu)	X33516-3	D7	Shubunkin of different tinge	X33060-3	E1
Bronzecoloured Fantail	X33667-4	F2	Hei zhen-zhu wen-yu	X33580-6	B4	Magpie (Panda) Dragoneye			Shubunkin, bluishblack	X33097-4	G1
Bubble-eye, black	X33309-6	H8	Hei-bai cai-se ji	X33097-4	G1	(Telescope)	X33388-4	D3	Shui-pao-yan	X33305-4	D8
Bubble-eye, calico	X33308-5	G8	Hibuna	X33059-3	B1	Magpie (Panda) Goldfish	X33086-3	C1	Subunkin	X33097-4	G1
Bubble-eye, red and black	X33307-4	F8	Hong	X33500-5	B5	Oranda, Jadehead variegated	X33523-5	F6	Suihogan	X33305-4	D8
Bubble-eye, red and white	X33306-4	E8	Hong-bai	X33579-3	C4	Oranda shishigashira	X33519-3	A6	Suihogan	X33307-4	F8
Bubble-eyes, red, red/ white,			Hong-bai hu-die wen-yu	X33414-5	B3	Oranda shishigashira	X33421-6	C5	Tancho deme(kin)	X33545-3	F5
red/black	X33305-4	D8	Hong-bai hu-tou	X33500-5	B5	Oranda shishigashira	X33520-5	C6	Tancho oranda shishigashira	X33411-5	E5
Cai-se feng-wei zhen-zhu	X33579-3	C4	Hong-bai lan-shou	X33600-6	A7	Oranda shishigashira	X33521-4	D6	Tancho Ranchu	X33517-3	E7
Cai-se gao-tou	X33435-4	H5	Hong-bai liu-qiu wen-yu	X33525-6	G3	Oranda shishigashira	X33522-5	E6	Tie-bao-qin long-jing gao-tou	X33521-4	D6
Cai-se ji	X33059-3	B1	Hong-bai yu-tou lan-shou	X33601-5	B7	Oranda shishigashira	X33515-4	G5	Tie-bao-qin mao-zi	X33520-5	C6
Cai-se ji	X33060-3	E1	Hong dan (rong) qiu	X33401-6	A8	Oranda, silver and red			Tosakin, black and yellow		
Cai-se lan-shou	X33400-6	H7	Hong-ding ma-nao yan	X33545-3	F5	lemon-headed	X33421-6	C5	(Curly-tailed Fantail)	X33556-5	F4
Cai-se liu-qiu wen-yu	X33526-4	H3	Hong-ding shi-zi-tou	X33517-3	E7	Oranda, blue	X33522-5	E6	Tosakin	X33556-5	F4
Cai-se long-jing	X33386-4	D2	Hong-hei gao-tou	X33520-5	C6	Oranda, brown	X33550-5	B6	Tosakin	X33557-5	G4
Cai-se shi-zi-tou	X33603-5	G7	Hong-hei hu-tou	X33519-3	A6	Oranda, calico	X33435-4	H5	Tosakin, red and black		
Cai-se shui-pao-yan	X33308-5	G8	Hong-hei ji	X33059-3	B1	Oranda, dragoneyed,			(Curly-tailed Fantail)	X33557-5	G4
Cai-se wen-yu	X33565-5	B2	Hong-hei long-jing	X33521-4	D6	red and black	X33521-4	D6	Tosakin, red with		
Cai-se yan-wei	X33306-4	F1	Hong-hei long-jing	X33387-4	E2	Oranda, purple	X33524-5	G6	white caudal borders	X33555-6	E4
Calico demekin	X33386-4	D2	Hong-hei long-jing	X33389-4	E3	Oranda, red and black	X33519-3	A6	Tosakin, silverish		
Celestial, red and black	X33446-3	C8	Hong-hei shui-pao-yan	X33307-4	F8	Oranda, red and white	X33500-5	B5	(Curly-tailed Fantail)	X33558-5	H4
Chairo Hanafusa	X33415-5	A4	Hong-hei wen-yu	X33566-5	C2	Oranda, red with			Tu-zuo jin wen-yu	X33555-6	E4
Chakin (Oranda)	X33550-5	B6	Hong-hei zhao-tian yan	X33446-3	C8	white fin borders	X33505-5	A5	Tu-zuo jin wen-yu	X33556-5	F4
Chakin Oranda	X33524-5	G6	Hong hu-tou	X33505-5	A5	Oranda, tripple coloured	X33510-4	D5	Tu-zuo jin wen-yu	X33557-5	G4
Chakin Perlscale	X33581-5	D4	Hong lan-shou	X33602-4	C7	Oranda, white, Lemon-headed	X33515-4	G5	Tu-zuo jin wen-yu	X33558-5	H4
Chotengan	X33446-3	C8	Hong lan-shou	X33604-5	H6	Panda Deme(kin)	X33388-4	D3	Veiltail, brown		
Comet, red and white (Sarasa)	X33085-3	D1	Hong long-jian ji	X33385-2	H1	Panda hibuna	X33086-3	C1	with red pompons	X33415-5	A4
Demekin	X33387-4	E2	Hong long-jing wen-yu	X33527-6	F3	Pearlscale, black	X33580-6	B4	Veiltail, calico	X33565-5	B2
Demekin	X33389-4	E3	Hong-tou bai long-jing	X33545-3	F5	Pearlscale, brown	X33581-5	D4	Veiltail, red and black	X33566-5	C2
Demekin funa	X33385-2	H1	Hong zhao-tian yan	X33445-3	B8	Pearlscales, red, white, calico	X33579-3	C4	Xi-que (hua) ji	X33086-3	C1
Dragoneye, calico			Hua hu-tou	X33421-6	C5	Ranchu	X33602-4	C7	Xi-que (hua) long-jing	X33388-4	D3
(Calico Telescope)	X33386-4	D2	Hua shui-pao-yan	X33306-4	E8	Ranchu	X33516-3	D7	Zi Gao-tou	X33550-5	B6
Dragoneye, red and black			Hua yan-wei ji	X33085-3	D1	Ranchu	X33604-5	H6	Zi hu-tou	X33524-5	G6
(Telescope)	X33387-4	E2	Huang hu-tou	X33515-4	G5	Ranchu, Jadehead red and white	X33601-5	B7	Zi wen-yu (rong) qiu	X33413-4	G2
Dragoneye, red and black			Jikin (Peakocktail)	X33425-4	A2	Ranchu, red and white	X33600-6	A7	Zi zhen-zhu wen-yu	X33581-5	D4
with high back	X33389-4	E3	Jikin	X33425-4	A2	Ranchu, red	X33602-4	C7	Zong (rong) qiu wen-yu	X33415-5	A4
Edonishiki	X33400-6	H7	Jin-yu (Jin-ji)	X33055-5	A1	Ranchu, red with			Zong wen-yu	X33667-4	F2
Eggfish, red with			Kaliko	X33565-5	B2	white caudal lobes	X33604-5	H6			
narial bouqet (pompons)	X33401-6	A8	Kaliko shishigashira	X33603-5	G7	Red Celestials	X33445-3	B8			
Fantail, brown			Kong-que ji	X33425-4	A2	Redcap, telescopeyed	X33545-3	F5			
with white and red pompon	X33413-4	G2	Kuro Perlscale	X33580-6	B4	Ryukin, calico	X33526-4	H3			

Symbols

Continent of origin:

Simply check the letter in front of the code-number

A = Africa   **E** = Europe   **N** = North America

S = South + Central America   **X** = Asia + Australia

Age:

the last number of the code always stands
for the age of the fish in the photo:

1 = small   (baby, juvenile colouration)
2 = medium   (young fish / saleable size)
3 = large   (half-grown / good saleable size)
4 = XL   (fully grown / adult)
5 = XXL   (brooder)
6 = show   (show-fish)

Immediate origin:

W = wild
B = bred
Z = breeding-form
X = crossbreed

Size:

..cm = approximate size these fish can reach as
adults

Sex:

♂ male   ♀ female   ♂♀ pair

Temperature:

◁ 18-22°C   (64 - 72°F)   (room temperature)
▷ 22-25°C   (72 -77°F)   (tropical fish)
△ 24-29°C   (75 - 85°F)   (Discus etc.)
▽ 10-22°C   (50 - 72°F)   cold

pH-Value:

⊕ pH 6,5 - 7,2 no special requirements (neutral)
↓P pH 5,8 - 6,5 prefers soft, slightly acidic water
↑P pH 7,5 - 8,5 prefers hard, alkaline water

Lighting:

○ bright, plenty of light / sun
◑ not too bright
● almost dark

Food:

☺ omnivorous / dry food, no special requirements
☺ food specialist, live food / frozen food
⊗ predator, feed with live fish
⊛ plant-eater, supplement with plant food

Swimming:

⊞ no special characteristics
⊤ in upper area / surface fish
⊥ in lower area / floor fish

Aquarium- set up:

▭ only floor and stones etc.
▧ stones / roots / crevices
▨ plant aquarium + stones / roots

Behaviour / reproduction:

♥ keep a pair or a trio
🐟 school fish, do not keep less than 10
🐟 egg-layer
🐟 livebearer / viviparous
🐟 mouthbrooder
🐟 cavebrooder
🐟 bubblenest-builder
◆ algae-eater, glass-cleaner (roots + spinach)
◇ non aggressive fish, easy to keep (mixed aquarium)
⚠ difficult to keep, read specialist literature beforehand
🛑 warning, extremely difficult, for experienced specialists only
𝟬 the eggs need special care
§ protected species (WA), special license required ("CITES")

Minimum tank: capacity:

		cm	litres
⌷ss⌷	super small	20 - 40 cm	5 - 20 l
⌷s⌷	small	40 - 80 cm	40 - 80 l
⌷m⌷	medium	60 - 100 cm	80 - 200 l
⌷l⌷	large	100 - 200 cm	200 - 400 l
⌷xl⌷	XL	200 - 400 cm	400 - 3000 l
⌷xxl⌷	XXL	over 400 cm	over 3000 l
			(show aquarium)

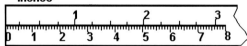

Inches / Centimeter ruler (0 - 8 cm, 0 - 3 inches)

Key to the abbreviations of the scientific names

Example:	**Belontia signata jonklaasi** Benl & Terofal, 1975	**ssp.:**	**Subspecies**
	Genus Species Subspecies Describer, Year of the publication		Explanation: Some species inhabit an area of very wide range; within this area, there are populations that differ significantly from other populations in appearance, but seen genetically, they belong nevertheless to the same species. Those populations get a third scientific name as geographical subspecies. If a subspecies name has not yet been formally given, the abbreviation spp. is added.
sp.:	**a species name is not yet available**		
sp. aff.:	**similar species**		
	The species is not yet determined but it is very similar to the one named in the following		
cf.:	**in all probability this species**	**var. :**	**Variation**
	The specimen shown or the respective population differs in some minor details from the typical form, but these differences don't justify to place it into a species of its own.		Explanation: Individual differences in colour combination, which are not fixed in geographical areas, are so-called variations. They do not get a special scientific name.
Hybrid :	**Crossbreed**	**Intergrade:**	**Mixed population of two subspecies**